GCC 5.2 GNU CPP Reference Manual

A catalogue record for this book is available from the Hong Kong Public Libraries.

Published in Hong Kong by Samurai Media Limited.

Email: info@samuraimedia.org

ISBN 978-988-8381-70-8

Table of Contents

1 Overview

The C preprocessor, often known as *cpp*, is a *macro processor* that is used automatically by the C compiler to transform your program before compilation. It is called a macro processor because it allows you to define *macros*, which are brief abbreviations for longer constructs.

The C preprocessor is intended to be used only with C, C++, and Objective-C source code. In the past, it has been abused as a general text processor. It will choke on input which does not obey C's lexical rules. For example, apostrophes will be interpreted as the beginning of character constants, and cause errors. Also, you cannot rely on it preserving characteristics of the input which are not significant to C-family languages. If a Makefile is preprocessed, all the hard tabs will be removed, and the Makefile will not work.

Having said that, you can often get away with using cpp on things which are not C. Other Algol-ish programming languages are often safe (Pascal, Ada, etc.) So is assembly, with caution. '-traditional-cpp' mode preserves more white space, and is otherwise more permissive. Many of the problems can be avoided by writing C or C++ style comments instead of native language comments, and keeping macros simple.

Wherever possible, you should use a preprocessor geared to the language you are writing in. Modern versions of the GNU assembler have macro facilities. Most high level programming languages have their own conditional compilation and inclusion mechanism. If all else fails, try a true general text processor, such as GNU M4.

C preprocessors vary in some details. This manual discusses the GNU C preprocessor, which provides a small superset of the features of ISO Standard C. In its default mode, the GNU C preprocessor does not do a few things required by the standard. These are features which are rarely, if ever, used, and may cause surprising changes to the meaning of a program which does not expect them. To get strict ISO Standard C, you should use the '-std=c90', '-std=c99' or '-std=c11' options, depending on which version of the standard you want. To get all the mandatory diagnostics, you must also use '-pedantic'. See Chapter 12 [Invocation], page 57.

This manual describes the behavior of the ISO preprocessor. To minimize gratuitous differences, where the ISO preprocessor's behavior does not conflict with traditional semantics, the traditional preprocessor should behave the same way. The various differences that do exist are detailed in the section Chapter 10 [Traditional Mode], page 49.

For clarity, unless noted otherwise, references to 'CPP' in this manual refer to GNU CPP.

1.1 Character sets

Source code character set processing in C and related languages is rather complicated. The C standard discusses two character sets, but there are really at least four.

The files input to CPP might be in any character set at all. CPP's very first action, before it even looks for line boundaries, is to convert the file into the character set it uses for internal processing. That set is what the C standard calls the *source* character set. It must be isomorphic with ISO 10646, also known as Unicode. CPP uses the UTF-8 encoding of Unicode.

The character sets of the input files are specified using the '-finput-charset=' option.

All preprocessing work (the subject of the rest of this manual) is carried out in the source character set. If you request textual output from the preprocessor with the '-E' option, it will be in UTF-8.

After preprocessing is complete, string and character constants are converted again, into the *execution* character set. This character set is under control of the user; the default is UTF-8, matching the source character set. Wide string and character constants have their own character set, which is not called out specifically in the standard. Again, it is under control of the user. The default is UTF-16 or UTF-32, whichever fits in the target's `wchar_t` type, in the target machine's byte order.[1] Octal and hexadecimal escape sequences do not undergo conversion; '\x12' has the value 0x12 regardless of the currently selected execution character set. All other escapes are replaced by the character in the source character set that they represent, then converted to the execution character set, just like unescaped characters.

In identifiers, characters outside the ASCII range can only be specified with the '\u' and '\U' escapes, not used directly. If strict ISO C90 conformance is specified with an option such as '-std=c90', or '-fno-extended-identifiers' is used, then those escapes are not permitted in identifiers.

1.2 Initial processing

The preprocessor performs a series of textual transformations on its input. These happen before all other processing. Conceptually, they happen in a rigid order, and the entire file is run through each transformation before the next one begins. CPP actually does them all at once, for performance reasons. These transformations correspond roughly to the first three "phases of translation" described in the C standard.

1. The input file is read into memory and broken into lines.

   Different systems use different conventions to indicate the end of a line. GCC accepts the ASCII control sequences *LF*, *CR LF* and *CR* as end-of-line markers. These are the canonical sequences used by Unix, DOS and VMS, and the classic Mac OS (before OSX) respectively. You may therefore safely copy source code written on any of those systems to a different one and use it without conversion. (GCC may lose track of the current line number if a file doesn't consistently use one convention, as sometimes happens when it is edited on computers with different conventions that share a network file system.)

   If the last line of any input file lacks an end-of-line marker, the end of the file is considered to implicitly supply one. The C standard says that this condition provokes undefined behavior, so GCC will emit a warning message.

2. If trigraphs are enabled, they are replaced by their corresponding single characters. By default GCC ignores trigraphs, but if you request a strictly conforming mode with the '-std' option, or you specify the '-trigraphs' option, then it converts them.

   These are nine three-character sequences, all starting with '??', that are defined by ISO C to stand for single characters. They permit obsolete systems that lack some of C's punctuation to use C. For example, '??/' stands for '\', so '??/n' is a character constant for a newline.

---

[1] UTF-16 does not meet the requirements of the C standard for a wide character set, but the choice of 16-bit `wchar_t` is enshrined in some system ABIs so we cannot fix this.

Trigraphs are not popular and many compilers implement them incorrectly. Portable code should not rely on trigraphs being either converted or ignored. With '-Wtrigraphs' GCC will warn you when a trigraph may change the meaning of your program if it were converted. See [Wtrigraphs], page 58.

In a string constant, you can prevent a sequence of question marks from being confused with a trigraph by inserting a backslash between the question marks, or by separating the string literal at the trigraph and making use of string literal concatenation. "(??\?)" is the string '(???)', not '(?]'. Traditional C compilers do not recognize these idioms.

The nine trigraphs and their replacements are

```
Trigraph:       ??(  ??)  ??<  ??>  ??=  ??/  ??'  ??!  ??-
Replacement:     [    ]    {    }    #    \    ^    |    ~
```

3. Continued lines are merged into one long line.

   A continued line is a line which ends with a backslash, '\'. The backslash is removed and the following line is joined with the current one. No space is inserted, so you may split a line anywhere, even in the middle of a word. (It is generally more readable to split lines only at white space.)

   The trailing backslash on a continued line is commonly referred to as a *backslash-newline*.

   If there is white space between a backslash and the end of a line, that is still a continued line. However, as this is usually the result of an editing mistake, and many compilers will not accept it as a continued line, GCC will warn you about it.

4. All comments are replaced with single spaces.

   There are two kinds of comments. *Block comments* begin with '/*' and continue until the next '*/'. Block comments do not nest:

   ```
   /* this is /* one comment */ text outside comment
   ```

   Line comments begin with '//' and continue to the end of the current line. Line comments do not nest either, but it does not matter, because they would end in the same place anyway.

   ```
   // this is // one comment
   text outside comment
   ```

   It is safe to put line comments inside block comments, or vice versa.

   ```
   /* block comment
      // contains line comment
      yet more comment
   */ outside comment

   // line comment /* contains block comment */
   ```

   But beware of commenting out one end of a block comment with a line comment.

   ```
   // l.c.  /* block comment begins
      oops! this isn't a comment anymore */
   ```

Comments are not recognized within string literals. "/* blah */" is the string constant '/* blah */', not an empty string.

Line comments are not in the 1989 edition of the C standard, but they are recognized by GCC as an extension. In C++ and in the 1999 edition of the C standard, they are an official part of the language.

Since these transformations happen before all other processing, you can split a line mechanically with backslash-newline anywhere. You can comment out the end of a line. You can continue a line comment onto the next line with backslash-newline. You can even split '/*', '*/', and '//' onto multiple lines with backslash-newline. For example:

```
/\
*
*/ # /*
*/ defi\
ne FO\
O 10\
20
```

is equivalent to #define FOO 1020. All these tricks are extremely confusing and should not be used in code intended to be readable.

There is no way to prevent a backslash at the end of a line from being interpreted as a backslash-newline. This cannot affect any correct program, however.

1.3 Tokenization

After the textual transformations are finished, the input file is converted into a sequence of *preprocessing tokens*. These mostly correspond to the syntactic tokens used by the C compiler, but there are a few differences. White space separates tokens; it is not itself a token of any kind. Tokens do not have to be separated by white space, but it is often necessary to avoid ambiguities.

When faced with a sequence of characters that has more than one possible tokenization, the preprocessor is greedy. It always makes each token, starting from the left, as big as possible before moving on to the next token. For instance, a+++++b is interpreted as a ++ ++ + b, not as a ++ + ++ b, even though the latter tokenization could be part of a valid C program and the former could not.

Once the input file is broken into tokens, the token boundaries never change, except when the '##' preprocessing operator is used to paste tokens together. See Section 3.5 [Concatenation], page 18. For example,

```
#define foo() bar
foo()baz
      ↦ bar baz
not
      ↦ barbaz
```

The compiler does not re-tokenize the preprocessor's output. Each preprocessing token becomes one compiler token.

Preprocessing tokens fall into five broad classes: identifiers, preprocessing numbers, string literals, punctuators, and other. An *identifier* is the same as an identifier in C: any sequence of letters, digits, or underscores, which begins with a letter or underscore. Keywords of C have no significance to the preprocessor; they are ordinary identifiers. You can define a macro whose name is a keyword, for instance. The only identifier which can be considered a preprocessing keyword is **defined**. See Section 4.2.3 [Defined], page 42.

This is mostly true of other languages which use the C preprocessor. However, a few of the keywords of C++ are significant even in the preprocessor. See Section 3.7.4 [C++ Named Operators], page 33.

In the 1999 C standard, identifiers may contain letters which are not part of the "basic source character set", at the implementation's discretion (such as accented Latin letters, Greek letters, or Chinese ideograms). This may be done with an extended character set, or the '\u' and '\U' escape sequences. GCC only accepts such characters in the '\u' and '\U' forms.

As an extension, GCC treats '$' as a letter. This is for compatibility with some systems, such as VMS, where '$' is commonly used in system-defined function and object names. '$' is not a letter in strictly conforming mode, or if you specify the '-$' option. See Chapter 12 [Invocation], page 57.

A *preprocessing number* has a rather bizarre definition. The category includes all the normal integer and floating point constants one expects of C, but also a number of other things one might not initially recognize as a number. Formally, preprocessing numbers begin with an optional period, a required decimal digit, and then continue with any sequence of letters, digits, underscores, periods, and exponents. Exponents are the two-character sequences 'e+', 'e-', 'E+', 'E-', 'p+', 'p-', 'P+', and 'P-'. (The exponents that begin with 'p' or 'P' are new to C99. They are used for hexadecimal floating-point constants.)

The purpose of this unusual definition is to isolate the preprocessor from the full complexity of numeric constants. It does not have to distinguish between lexically valid and invalid floating-point numbers, which is complicated. The definition also permits you to split an identifier at any position and get exactly two tokens, which can then be pasted back together with the '##' operator.

It's possible for preprocessing numbers to cause programs to be misinterpreted. For example, `0xE+12` is a preprocessing number which does not translate to any valid numeric constant, therefore a syntax error. It does not mean `0xE + 12`, which is what you might have intended.

String literals are string constants, character constants, and header file names (the argument of '`#include`').[2] String constants and character constants are straightforward: "..." or '...'. In either case embedded quotes should be escaped with a backslash: '\'' is the character constant for '''. There is no limit on the length of a character constant, but the value of a character constant that contains more than one character is implementation-defined. See Chapter 11 [Implementation Details], page 52.

Header file names either look like string constants, "...", or are written with angle brackets instead, <...>. In either case, backslash is an ordinary character. There is no way to escape the closing quote or angle bracket. The preprocessor looks for the header file in different places depending on which form you use. See Section 2.2 [Include Operation], page 8.

No string literal may extend past the end of a line. Older versions of GCC accepted multi-line string constants. You may use continued lines instead, or string constant concatenation. See Section 11.4 [Differences from previous versions], page 56.

Punctuators are all the usual bits of punctuation which are meaningful to C and C++. All but three of the punctuation characters in ASCII are C punctuators. The exceptions are '@', '$', and ' ' '. In addition, all the two- and three-character operators are punctuators. There are also six *digraphs*, which the C++ standard calls *alternative tokens*, which are merely

---

[2] The C standard uses the term *string literal* to refer only to what we are calling *string constants*.

alternate ways to spell other punctuators. This is a second attempt to work around missing punctuation in obsolete systems. It has no negative side effects, unlike trigraphs, but does not cover as much ground. The digraphs and their corresponding normal punctuators are:

```
Digraph:        <%  %>  <:   :>  %:   %:%:
Punctuator:      {   }   [   ]   #    ##
```

Any other single character is considered "other". It is passed on to the preprocessor's output unmolested. The C compiler will almost certainly reject source code containing "other" tokens. In ASCII, the only other characters are '@', '$', '`', and control characters other than NUL (all bits zero). (Note that '$' is normally considered a letter.) All characters with the high bit set (numeric range 0x7F–0xFF) are also "other" in the present implementation. This will change when proper support for international character sets is added to GCC.

NUL is a special case because of the high probability that its appearance is accidental, and because it may be invisible to the user (many terminals do not display NUL at all). Within comments, NULs are silently ignored, just as any other character would be. In running text, NUL is considered white space. For example, these two directives have the same meaning.

```
#define X^@1
#define X 1
```

(where '^@' is ASCII NUL). Within string or character constants, NULs are preserved. In the latter two cases the preprocessor emits a warning message.

1.4 The preprocessing language

After tokenization, the stream of tokens may simply be passed straight to the compiler's parser. However, if it contains any operations in the *preprocessing language*, it will be transformed first. This stage corresponds roughly to the standard's "translation phase 4" and is what most people think of as the preprocessor's job.

The preprocessing language consists of *directives* to be executed and *macros* to be expanded. Its primary capabilities are:

- Inclusion of header files. These are files of declarations that can be substituted into your program.

- Macro expansion. You can define *macros*, which are abbreviations for arbitrary fragments of C code. The preprocessor will replace the macros with their definitions throughout the program. Some macros are automatically defined for you.

- Conditional compilation. You can include or exclude parts of the program according to various conditions.

- Line control. If you use a program to combine or rearrange source files into an intermediate file which is then compiled, you can use line control to inform the compiler where each source line originally came from.

- Diagnostics. You can detect problems at compile time and issue errors or warnings.

There are a few more, less useful, features.

Except for expansion of predefined macros, all these operations are triggered with *preprocessing directives*. Preprocessing directives are lines in your program that start with '#'. Whitespace is allowed before and after the '#'. The '#' is followed by an identifier, the *directive name*. It specifies the operation to perform. Directives are commonly referred to as '`#name`' where *name* is the directive name. For example, '`#define`' is the directive that defines a macro.

The '`#`' which begins a directive cannot come from a macro expansion. Also, the directive name is not macro expanded. Thus, if `foo` is defined as a macro expanding to `define`, that does not make '`#foo`' a valid preprocessing directive.

The set of valid directive names is fixed. Programs cannot define new preprocessing directives.

Some directives require arguments; these make up the rest of the directive line and must be separated from the directive name by whitespace. For example, '`#define`' must be followed by a macro name and the intended expansion of the macro.

A preprocessing directive cannot cover more than one line. The line may, however, be continued with backslash-newline, or by a block comment which extends past the end of the line. In either case, when the directive is processed, the continuations have already been merged with the first line to make one long line.

2 Header Files

A header file is a file containing C declarations and macro definitions (see Chapter 3 [Macros], page 13) to be shared between several source files. You request the use of a header file in your program by *including* it, with the C preprocessing directive '`#include`'.

Header files serve two purposes.

- System header files declare the interfaces to parts of the operating system. You include them in your program to supply the definitions and declarations you need to invoke system calls and libraries.

- Your own header files contain declarations for interfaces between the source files of your program. Each time you have a group of related declarations and macro definitions all or most of which are needed in several different source files, it is a good idea to create a header file for them.

Including a header file produces the same results as copying the header file into each source file that needs it. Such copying would be time-consuming and error-prone. With a header file, the related declarations appear in only one place. If they need to be changed, they can be changed in one place, and programs that include the header file will automatically use the new version when next recompiled. The header file eliminates the labor of finding and changing all the copies as well as the risk that a failure to find one copy will result in inconsistencies within a program.

In C, the usual convention is to give header files names that end with '`.h`'. It is most portable to use only letters, digits, dashes, and underscores in header file names, and at most one dot.

2.1 Include Syntax

Both user and system header files are included using the preprocessing directive '`#include`'. It has two variants:

```
#include <file>
```
> This variant is used for system header files. It searches for a file named *file* in a standard list of system directories. You can prepend directories to this list with the '-I' option (see Chapter 12 [Invocation], page 57).

```
#include "file"
```
> This variant is used for header files of your own program. It searches for a file named *file* first in the directory containing the current file, then in the quote directories and then the same directories used for `<file>`. You can prepend directories to the list of quote directories with the '-iquote' option.

The argument of '#include', whether delimited with quote marks or angle brackets, behaves like a string constant in that comments are not recognized, and macro names are not expanded. Thus, `#include <x/*y>` specifies inclusion of a system header file named 'x/*y'.

However, if backslashes occur within *file*, they are considered ordinary text characters, not escape characters. None of the character escape sequences appropriate to string constants in C are processed. Thus, `#include "x\n\\y"` specifies a filename containing three backslashes. (Some systems interpret '\' as a pathname separator. All of these also interpret '/' the same way. It is most portable to use only '/'.)

It is an error if there is anything (other than comments) on the line after the file name.

2.2 Include Operation

The '#include' directive works by directing the C preprocessor to scan the specified file as input before continuing with the rest of the current file. The output from the preprocessor contains the output already generated, followed by the output resulting from the included file, followed by the output that comes from the text after the '#include' directive. For example, if you have a header file 'header.h' as follows,

```
char *test (void);
```

and a main program called 'program.c' that uses the header file, like this,

```
int x;
#include "header.h"

int
main (void)
{
  puts (test ());
}
```

the compiler will see the same token stream as it would if 'program.c' read

```
int x;
char *test (void);

int
main (void)
{
  puts (test ());
}
```

Included files are not limited to declarations and macro definitions; those are merely the typical uses. Any fragment of a C program can be included from another file. The include file could even contain the beginning of a statement that is concluded in the containing file, or the end of a statement that was started in the including file. However, an included file must consist of complete tokens. Comments and string literals which have not been closed by the end of an included file are invalid. For error recovery, they are considered to end at the end of the file.

To avoid confusion, it is best if header files contain only complete syntactic units—function declarations or definitions, type declarations, etc.

The line following the '#include' directive is always treated as a separate line by the C preprocessor, even if the included file lacks a final newline.

2.3 Search Path

GCC looks in several different places for headers. On a normal Unix system, if you do not instruct it otherwise, it will look for headers requested with #include <*file*> in:

```
/usr/local/include
libdir/gcc/target/version/include
/usr/target/include
/usr/include
```

For C++ programs, it will also look in '*libdir*/../include/c++/*version*', first. In the above, *target* is the canonical name of the system GCC was configured to compile code for; often but not always the same as the canonical name of the system it runs on. *version* is the version of GCC in use.

You can add to this list with the '-I*dir*' command-line option. All the directories named by '-I' are searched, in left-to-right order, *before* the default directories. The only exception is when 'dir' is already searched by default. In this case, the option is ignored and the search order for system directories remains unchanged.

Duplicate directories are removed from the quote and bracket search chains before the two chains are merged to make the final search chain. Thus, it is possible for a directory to occur twice in the final search chain if it was specified in both the quote and bracket chains.

You can prevent GCC from searching any of the default directories with the '-nostdinc' option. This is useful when you are compiling an operating system kernel or some other program that does not use the standard C library facilities, or the standard C library itself. '-I' options are not ignored as described above when '-nostdinc' is in effect.

GCC looks for headers requested with #include "*file*" first in the directory containing the current file, then in the directories as specified by '-iquote' options, then in the same places it would have looked for a header requested with angle brackets. For example, if '/usr/include/sys/stat.h' contains #include "types.h", GCC looks for 'types.h' first in '/usr/include/sys', then in its usual search path.

'#line' (see Chapter 6 [Line Control], page 45) does not change GCC's idea of the directory containing the current file.

You may put '-I-' at any point in your list of '-I' options. This has two effects. First, directories appearing before the '-I-' in the list are searched only for headers requested with quote marks. Directories after '-I-' are searched for all headers. Second, the directory containing the current file is not searched for anything, unless it happens to be one of the directories named by an '-I' switch. '-I-' is deprecated, '-iquote' should be used instead.

'-I. -I-' is not the same as no '-I' options at all, and does not cause the same behavior for '<>' includes that '""' includes get with no special options. '-I.' searches the compiler's current working directory for header files. That may or may not be the same as the directory containing the current file.

If you need to look for headers in a directory named '-', write '-I./-'.

There are several more ways to adjust the header search path. They are generally less useful. See Chapter 12 [Invocation], page 57.

2.4 Once-Only Headers

If a header file happens to be included twice, the compiler will process its contents twice. This is very likely to cause an error, e.g. when the compiler sees the same structure definition twice. Even if it does not, it will certainly waste time.

The standard way to prevent this is to enclose the entire real contents of the file in a conditional, like this:

```
/* File foo.  */
#ifndef FILE_FOO_SEEN
#define FILE_FOO_SEEN

the entire file

#endif /* !FILE_FOO_SEEN */
```

This construct is commonly known as a *wrapper #ifndef*. When the header is included again, the conditional will be false, because FILE_FOO_SEEN is defined. The preprocessor will skip over the entire contents of the file, and the compiler will not see it twice.

CPP optimizes even further. It remembers when a header file has a wrapper '#ifndef'. If a subsequent '#include' specifies that header, and the macro in the '#ifndef' is still defined, it does not bother to rescan the file at all.

You can put comments outside the wrapper. They will not interfere with this optimization.

The macro FILE_FOO_SEEN is called the *controlling macro* or *guard macro*. In a user header file, the macro name should not begin with '_'. In a system header file, it should begin with '__' to avoid conflicts with user programs. In any kind of header file, the macro name should contain the name of the file and some additional text, to avoid conflicts with other header files.

2.5 Alternatives to Wrapper #ifndef

CPP supports two more ways of indicating that a header file should be read only once. Neither one is as portable as a wrapper '#ifndef' and we recommend you do not use them in new programs, with the caveat that '#import' is standard practice in Objective-C.

CPP supports a variant of '#include' called '#import' which includes a file, but does so at most once. If you use '#import' instead of '#include', then you don't need the conditionals inside the header file to prevent multiple inclusion of the contents. '#import' is standard in Objective-C, but is considered a deprecated extension in C and C++.

'#import' is not a well designed feature. It requires the users of a header file to know that it should only be included once. It is much better for the header file's implementor to write the file so that users don't need to know this. Using a wrapper '#ifndef' accomplishes this goal.

In the present implementation, a single use of '#import' will prevent the file from ever being read again, by either '#import' or '#include'. You should not rely on this; do not use both '#import' and '#include' to refer to the same header file.

Another way to prevent a header file from being included more than once is with the '#pragma once' directive. If '#pragma once' is seen when scanning a header file, that file will never be read again, no matter what.

'#pragma once' does not have the problems that '#import' does, but it is not recognized by all preprocessors, so you cannot rely on it in a portable program.

2.6 Computed Includes

Sometimes it is necessary to select one of several different header files to be included into your program. They might specify configuration parameters to be used on different sorts of operating systems, for instance. You could do this with a series of conditionals,

```
#if SYSTEM_1
# include "system_1.h"
#elif SYSTEM_2
# include "system_2.h"
#elif SYSTEM_3
  ...
#endif
```

That rapidly becomes tedious. Instead, the preprocessor offers the ability to use a macro for the header name. This is called a *computed include*. Instead of writing a header name as the direct argument of '#include', you simply put a macro name there instead:

```
#define SYSTEM_H "system_1.h"
  ...
#include SYSTEM_H
```

SYSTEM_H will be expanded, and the preprocessor will look for 'system_1.h' as if the '#include' had been written that way originally. SYSTEM_H could be defined by your Makefile with a '-D' option.

You must be careful when you define the macro. '#define' saves tokens, not text. The preprocessor has no way of knowing that the macro will be used as the argument of '#include', so it generates ordinary tokens, not a header name. This is unlikely to cause problems if you use double-quote includes, which are close enough to string constants. If you use angle brackets, however, you may have trouble.

The syntax of a computed include is actually a bit more general than the above. If the first non-whitespace character after '#include' is not '"' or '<', then the entire line is macro-expanded like running text would be.

If the line expands to a single string constant, the contents of that string constant are the file to be included. CPP does not re-examine the string for embedded quotes, but neither does it process backslash escapes in the string. Therefore

```
#define HEADER "a\"b"
#include HEADER
```

looks for a file named 'a\"b'. CPP searches for the file according to the rules for double-quoted includes.

If the line expands to a token stream beginning with a '<' token and including a '>' token, then the tokens between the '<' and the first '>' are combined to form the filename to be included. Any whitespace between tokens is reduced to a single space; then any space after the initial '<' is retained, but a trailing space before the closing '>' is ignored. CPP searches for the file according to the rules for angle-bracket includes.

In either case, if there are any tokens on the line after the file name, an error occurs and the directive is not processed. It is also an error if the result of expansion does not match either of the two expected forms.

These rules are implementation-defined behavior according to the C standard. To minimize the risk of different compilers interpreting your computed includes differently, we recommend you use only a single object-like macro which expands to a string constant. This will also minimize confusion for people reading your program.

2.7 Wrapper Headers

Sometimes it is necessary to adjust the contents of a system-provided header file without editing it directly. GCC's `fixincludes` operation does this, for example. One way to do that would be to create a new header file with the same name and insert it in the search path before the original header. That works fine as long as you're willing to replace the old header entirely. But what if you want to refer to the old header from the new one?

You cannot simply include the old header with '#include'. That will start from the beginning, and find your new header again. If your header is not protected from multiple inclusion (see Section 2.4 [Once-Only Headers], page 10), it will recurse infinitely and cause a fatal error.

You could include the old header with an absolute pathname:

```
#include "/usr/include/old-header.h"
```

This works, but is not clean; should the system headers ever move, you would have to edit the new headers to match.

There is no way to solve this problem within the C standard, but you can use the GNU extension '#include_next'. It means, "Include the *next* file with this name". This directive works like '#include' except in searching for the specified file: it starts searching the list of header file directories *after* the directory in which the current file was found.

Suppose you specify '-I /usr/local/include', and the list of directories to search also includes '/usr/include'; and suppose both directories contain 'signal.h'. Ordinary #include <signal.h> finds the file under '/usr/local/include'. If that file contains #include_next <signal.h>, it starts searching after that directory, and finds the file in '/usr/include'.

'#include_next' does not distinguish between <file> and "file" inclusion, nor does it check that the file you specify has the same name as the current file. It simply looks for the file named, starting with the directory in the search path after the one where the current file was found.

The use of '#include_next' can lead to great confusion. We recommend it be used only when there is no other alternative. In particular, it should not be used in the headers belonging to a specific program; it should be used only to make global corrections along the lines of fixincludes.

2.8 System Headers

The header files declaring interfaces to the operating system and runtime libraries often cannot be written in strictly conforming C. Therefore, GCC gives code found in *system headers* special treatment. All warnings, other than those generated by '#warning' (see Chapter 5 [Diagnostics], page 44), are suppressed while GCC is processing a system header. Macros defined in a system header are immune to a few warnings wherever they are expanded. This immunity is granted on an ad-hoc basis, when we find that a warning generates lots of false positives because of code in macros defined in system headers.

Normally, only the headers found in specific directories are considered system headers. These directories are determined when GCC is compiled. There are, however, two ways to make normal headers into system headers.

The '-isystem' command-line option adds its argument to the list of directories to search for headers, just like '-I'. Any headers found in that directory will be considered system headers.

All directories named by '-isystem' are searched *after* all directories named by '-I', no matter what their order was on the command line. If the same directory is named by both '-I' and '-isystem', the '-I' option is ignored. GCC provides an informative message when this occurs if '-v' is used.

There is also a directive, #pragma GCC system_header, which tells GCC to consider the rest of the current include file a system header, no matter where it was found. Code that comes before the '#pragma' in the file will not be affected. #pragma GCC system_header has no effect in the primary source file.

On very old systems, some of the pre-defined system header directories get even more special treatment. GNU C++ considers code in headers found in those directories to be surrounded by an extern "C" block. There is no way to request this behavior with a '#pragma', or from the command line.

3 Macros

A *macro* is a fragment of code which has been given a name. Whenever the name is used, it is replaced by the contents of the macro. There are two kinds of macros. They differ mostly in what they look like when they are used. *Object-like* macros resemble data objects when used, *function-like* macros resemble function calls.

You may define any valid identifier as a macro, even if it is a C keyword. The preprocessor does not know anything about keywords. This can be useful if you wish to hide a keyword such as const from an older compiler that does not understand it. However, the preprocessor operator defined (see Section 4.2.3 [Defined], page 42) can never be defined as a macro, and C++'s named operators (see Section 3.7.4 [C++ Named Operators], page 33) cannot be macros when you are compiling C++.

3.1 Object-like Macros

An *object-like macro* is a simple identifier which will be replaced by a code fragment. It is called object-like because it looks like a data object in code that uses it. They are most commonly used to give symbolic names to numeric constants.

You create macros with the '#define' directive. '#define' is followed by the name of the macro and then the token sequence it should be an abbreviation for, which is variously referred to as the macro's *body*, *expansion* or *replacement list*. For example,

```
#define BUFFER_SIZE 1024
```

defines a macro named BUFFER_SIZE as an abbreviation for the token 1024. If somewhere after this '#define' directive there comes a C statement of the form

```
foo = (char *) malloc (BUFFER_SIZE);
```

then the C preprocessor will recognize and *expand* the macro BUFFER_SIZE. The C compiler will see the same tokens as it would if you had written

```
foo = (char *) malloc (1024);
```

By convention, macro names are written in uppercase. Programs are easier to read when it is possible to tell at a glance which names are macros.

The macro's body ends at the end of the '#define' line. You may continue the definition onto multiple lines, if necessary, using backslash-newline. When the macro is expanded, however, it will all come out on one line. For example,

```
#define NUMBERS 1, \
                2, \
                3
int x[] = { NUMBERS };
     ↦ int x[] = { 1, 2, 3 };
```

The most common visible consequence of this is surprising line numbers in error messages.

There is no restriction on what can go in a macro body provided it decomposes into valid preprocessing tokens. Parentheses need not balance, and the body need not resemble valid C code. (If it does not, you may get error messages from the C compiler when you use the macro.)

The C preprocessor scans your program sequentially. Macro definitions take effect at the place you write them. Therefore, the following input to the C preprocessor

```
foo = X;
#define X 4
bar = X;
```

produces

```
foo = X;
bar = 4;
```

When the preprocessor expands a macro name, the macro's expansion replaces the macro invocation, then the expansion is examined for more macros to expand. For example,

```
#define TABLESIZE BUFSIZE
#define BUFSIZE 1024
TABLESIZE
     ↦ BUFSIZE
     ↦ 1024
```

TABLESIZE is expanded first to produce BUFSIZE, then that macro is expanded to produce the final result, 1024.

Notice that BUFSIZE was not defined when TABLESIZE was defined. The '#define' for TABLESIZE uses exactly the expansion you specify—in this case, BUFSIZE—and does not check to see whether it too contains macro names. Only when you *use* TABLESIZE is the result of its expansion scanned for more macro names.

This makes a difference if you change the definition of `BUFSIZE` at some point in the source file. `TABLESIZE`, defined as shown, will always expand using the definition of `BUFSIZE` that is currently in effect:

```
#define BUFSIZE 1020
#define TABLESIZE BUFSIZE
#undef BUFSIZE
#define BUFSIZE 37
```

Now `TABLESIZE` expands (in two stages) to `37`.

If the expansion of a macro contains its own name, either directly or via intermediate macros, it is not expanded again when the expansion is examined for more macros. This prevents infinite recursion. See Section 3.10.5 [Self-Referential Macros], page 37, for the precise details.

3.2 Function-like Macros

You can also define macros whose use looks like a function call. These are called *function-like macros*. To define a function-like macro, you use the same '`#define`' directive, but you put a pair of parentheses immediately after the macro name. For example,

```
#define lang_init()  c_init()
lang_init()
      ↦ c_init()
```

A function-like macro is only expanded if its name appears with a pair of parentheses after it. If you write just the name, it is left alone. This can be useful when you have a function and a macro of the same name, and you wish to use the function sometimes.

```
extern void foo(void);
#define foo() /* optimized inline version */
...
  foo();
  funcptr = foo;
```

Here the call to `foo()` will use the macro, but the function pointer will get the address of the real function. If the macro were to be expanded, it would cause a syntax error.

If you put spaces between the macro name and the parentheses in the macro definition, that does not define a function-like macro, it defines an object-like macro whose expansion happens to begin with a pair of parentheses.

```
#define lang_init ()    c_init()
lang_init()
      ↦ () c_init()()
```

The first two pairs of parentheses in this expansion come from the macro. The third is the pair that was originally after the macro invocation. Since `lang_init` is an object-like macro, it does not consume those parentheses.

3.3 Macro Arguments

Function-like macros can take *arguments*, just like true functions. To define a macro that uses arguments, you insert *parameters* between the pair of parentheses in the macro definition that make the macro function-like. The parameters must be valid C identifiers, separated by commas and optionally whitespace.

To invoke a macro that takes arguments, you write the name of the macro followed by a list of *actual arguments* in parentheses, separated by commas. The invocation of the macro need not be restricted to a single logical line—it can cross as many lines in the source file as you wish. The number of arguments you give must match the number of parameters in the macro definition. When the macro is expanded, each use of a parameter in its body is replaced by the tokens of the corresponding argument. (You need not use all of the parameters in the macro body.)

As an example, here is a macro that computes the minimum of two numeric values, as it is defined in many C programs, and some uses.

```
#define min(X, Y)  ((X) < (Y) ? (X) : (Y))
  x = min(a, b);           ↦   x = ((a) < (b) ? (a) : (b));
  y = min(1, 2);           ↦   y = ((1) < (2) ? (1) : (2));
  z = min(a + 28, *p);     ↦   z = ((a + 28) < (*p) ? (a + 28) : (*p));
```

(In this small example you can already see several of the dangers of macro arguments. See Section 3.10 [Macro Pitfalls], page 35, for detailed explanations.)

Leading and trailing whitespace in each argument is dropped, and all whitespace between the tokens of an argument is reduced to a single space. Parentheses within each argument must balance; a comma within such parentheses does not end the argument. However, there is no requirement for square brackets or braces to balance, and they do not prevent a comma from separating arguments. Thus,

```
macro (array[x = y, x + 1])
```

passes two arguments to macro: `array[x = y` and `x + 1]`. If you want to supply `array[x = y, x + 1]` as an argument, you can write it as `array[(x = y, x + 1)]`, which is equivalent C code.

All arguments to a macro are completely macro-expanded before they are substituted into the macro body. After substitution, the complete text is scanned again for macros to expand, including the arguments. This rule may seem strange, but it is carefully designed so you need not worry about whether any function call is actually a macro invocation. You can run into trouble if you try to be too clever, though. See Section 3.10.6 [Argument Prescan], page 38, for detailed discussion.

For example, `min (min (a, b), c)` is first expanded to

```
min (((a) < (b) ? (a) : (b)), (c))
```

and then to

```
((((a) < (b) ? (a) : (b))) < (c)
 ? (((a) < (b) ? (a) : (b)))
 : (c))
```

(Line breaks shown here for clarity would not actually be generated.)

You can leave macro arguments empty; this is not an error to the preprocessor (but many macros will then expand to invalid code). You cannot leave out arguments entirely; if a macro takes two arguments, there must be exactly one comma at the top level of its argument list. Here are some silly examples using min:

```
min(, b)        ↦  ((   ) < (b) ? (   ) : (b))
min(a, )        ↦  ((a  ) < ( ) ? (a  ) : ( ))
min(,)          ↦  ((   ) < ( ) ? (   ) : ( ))
min((,),)       ↦  (((,)) < ( ) ? ((,)) : ( ))

min()        error   macro "min" requires 2 arguments, but only 1 given
min(,,)      error   macro "min" passed 3 arguments, but takes just 2
```

Whitespace is not a preprocessing token, so if a macro `foo` takes one argument, `foo ()` and `foo ( )` both supply it an empty argument. Previous GNU preprocessor implementations and documentation were incorrect on this point, insisting that a function-like macro that takes a single argument be passed a space if an empty argument was required.

Macro parameters appearing inside string literals are not replaced by their corresponding actual arguments.

```
#define foo(x) x, "x"
foo(bar)        ↦ bar, "x"
```

3.4 Stringification

Sometimes you may want to convert a macro argument into a string constant. Parameters are not replaced inside string constants, but you can use the '#' preprocessing operator instead. When a macro parameter is used with a leading '#', the preprocessor replaces it with the literal text of the actual argument, converted to a string constant. Unlike normal parameter replacement, the argument is not macro-expanded first. This is called *stringification*.

There is no way to combine an argument with surrounding text and stringify it all together. Instead, you can write a series of adjacent string constants and stringified arguments. The preprocessor will replace the stringified arguments with string constants. The C compiler will then combine all the adjacent string constants into one long string.

Here is an example of a macro definition that uses stringification:

```
#define WARN_IF(EXP) \
do { if (EXP) \
        fprintf (stderr, "Warning: " #EXP "\n"); } \
while (0)
WARN_IF (x == 0);
    ↦ do { if (x == 0)
            fprintf (stderr, "Warning: " "x == 0" "\n"); } while (0);
```

The argument for `EXP` is substituted once, as-is, into the `if` statement, and once, stringified, into the argument to `fprintf`. If `x` were a macro, it would be expanded in the `if` statement, but not in the string.

The `do` and `while (0)` are a kludge to make it possible to write `WARN_IF (arg);`, which the resemblance of `WARN_IF` to a function would make C programmers want to do; see Section 3.10.3 [Swallowing the Semicolon], page 36.

Stringification in C involves more than putting double-quote characters around the fragment. The preprocessor backslash-escapes the quotes surrounding embedded string constants, and all backslashes within string and character constants, in order to get a valid C string constant with the proper contents. Thus, stringifying `p = "foo\n";` results in `"p = \"foo\\n\";"`. However, backslashes that are not inside string or character constants are not duplicated: '\n' by itself stringifies to `"\n"`.

All leading and trailing whitespace in text being stringified is ignored. Any sequence of whitespace in the middle of the text is converted to a single space in the stringified result. Comments are replaced by whitespace long before stringification happens, so they never appear in stringified text.

There is no way to convert a macro argument into a character constant.

If you want to stringify the result of expansion of a macro argument, you have to use two levels of macros.

```
#define xstr(s) str(s)
#define str(s) #s
#define foo 4
str (foo)
      ↦ "foo"
xstr (foo)
      ↦ xstr (4)
      ↦ str (4)
      ↦ "4"
```

`s` is stringified when it is used in `str`, so it is not macro-expanded first. But `s` is an ordinary argument to `xstr`, so it is completely macro-expanded before `xstr` itself is expanded (see Section 3.10.6 [Argument Prescan], page 38). Therefore, by the time `str` gets to its argument, it has already been macro-expanded.

3.5 Concatenation

It is often useful to merge two tokens into one while expanding macros. This is called *token pasting* or *token concatenation*. The '`##`' preprocessing operator performs token pasting. When a macro is expanded, the two tokens on either side of each '`##`' operator are combined into a single token, which then replaces the '`##`' and the two original tokens in the macro expansion. Usually both will be identifiers, or one will be an identifier and the other a preprocessing number. When pasted, they make a longer identifier. This isn't the only valid case. It is also possible to concatenate two numbers (or a number and a name, such as `1.5` and `e3`) into a number. Also, multi-character operators such as `+=` can be formed by token pasting.

However, two tokens that don't together form a valid token cannot be pasted together. For example, you cannot concatenate `x` with `+` in either order. If you try, the preprocessor issues a warning and emits the two tokens. Whether it puts white space between the tokens is undefined. It is common to find unnecessary uses of '`##`' in complex macros. If you get this warning, it is likely that you can simply remove the '`##`'.

Both the tokens combined by '`##`' could come from the macro body, but you could just as well write them as one token in the first place. Token pasting is most useful when one or both of the tokens comes from a macro argument. If either of the tokens next to an '`##`' is a parameter name, it is replaced by its actual argument before '`##`' executes. As with stringification, the actual argument is not macro-expanded first. If the argument is empty, that '`##`' has no effect.

Keep in mind that the C preprocessor converts comments to whitespace before macros are even considered. Therefore, you cannot create a comment by concatenating '`/`' and '`*`'. You can put as much whitespace between '`##`' and its operands as you like, including comments, and you can put comments in arguments that will be concatenated. However, it is an error if '`##`' appears at either end of a macro body.

Consider a C program that interprets named commands. There probably needs to be a table of commands, perhaps an array of structures declared as follows:

```
struct command
{
  char *name;
  void (*function) (void);
};

struct command commands[] =
{
  { "quit", quit_command },
  { "help", help_command },
  ...
};
```

It would be cleaner not to have to give each command name twice, once in the string constant and once in the function name. A macro which takes the name of a command as an argument can make this unnecessary. The string constant can be created with stringification, and the function name by concatenating the argument with '_command'. Here is how it is done:

```
#define COMMAND(NAME)  { #NAME, NAME ## _command }

struct command commands[] =
{
  COMMAND (quit),
  COMMAND (help),
  ...
};
```

3.6 Variadic Macros

A macro can be declared to accept a variable number of arguments much as a function can. The syntax for defining the macro is similar to that of a function. Here is an example:

```
#define eprintf(...) fprintf (stderr, __VA_ARGS__)
```

This kind of macro is called *variadic*. When the macro is invoked, all the tokens in its argument list after the last named argument (this macro has none), including any commas, become the *variable argument*. This sequence of tokens replaces the identifier `__VA_ARGS__` in the macro body wherever it appears. Thus, we have this expansion:

```
eprintf ("%s:%d: ", input_file, lineno)
     ↦  fprintf (stderr, "%s:%d: ", input_file, lineno)
```

The variable argument is completely macro-expanded before it is inserted into the macro expansion, just like an ordinary argument. You may use the '#' and '##' operators to stringify the variable argument or to paste its leading or trailing token with another token. (But see below for an important special case for '##'.)

If your macro is complicated, you may want a more descriptive name for the variable argument than `__VA_ARGS__`. CPP permits this, as an extension. You may write an argument name immediately before the '. . .'; that name is used for the variable argument. The `eprintf` macro above could be written

```
#define eprintf(args...) fprintf (stderr, args)
```

using this extension. You cannot use `__VA_ARGS__` and this extension in the same macro.

You can have named arguments as well as variable arguments in a variadic macro. We could define `eprintf` like this, instead:

```
#define eprintf(format, ...) fprintf (stderr, format, __VA_ARGS__)
```

This formulation looks more descriptive, but unfortunately it is less flexible: you must now supply at least one argument after the format string. In standard C, you cannot omit the comma separating the named argument from the variable arguments. Furthermore, if you leave the variable argument empty, you will get a syntax error, because there will be an extra comma after the format string.

```
eprintf("success!\n", );
        ↦ fprintf(stderr, "success!\n", );
```

GNU CPP has a pair of extensions which deal with this problem. First, you are allowed to leave the variable argument out entirely:

```
eprintf ("success!\n")
        ↦ fprintf(stderr, "success!\n", );
```

Second, the '##' token paste operator has a special meaning when placed between a comma and a variable argument. If you write

```
#define eprintf(format, ...) fprintf (stderr, format, ##__VA_ARGS__)
```

and the variable argument is left out when the eprintf macro is used, then the comma before the '##' will be deleted. This does *not* happen if you pass an empty argument, nor does it happen if the token preceding '##' is anything other than a comma.

```
eprintf ("success!\n")
        ↦ fprintf(stderr, "success!\n");
```

The above explanation is ambiguous about the case where the only macro parameter is a variable arguments parameter, as it is meaningless to try to distinguish whether no argument at all is an empty argument or a missing argument. In this case the C99 standard is clear that the comma must remain, however the existing GCC extension used to swallow the comma. So CPP retains the comma when conforming to a specific C standard, and drops it otherwise.

C99 mandates that the only place the identifier __VA_ARGS__ can appear is in the replacement list of a variadic macro. It may not be used as a macro name, macro argument name, or within a different type of macro. It may also be forbidden in open text; the standard is ambiguous. We recommend you avoid using it except for its defined purpose.

Variadic macros are a new feature in C99. GNU CPP has supported them for a long time, but only with a named variable argument ('args...', not '...' and __VA_ARGS__). If you are concerned with portability to previous versions of GCC, you should use only named variable arguments. On the other hand, if you are concerned with portability to other conforming implementations of C99, you should use only __VA_ARGS__.

Previous versions of CPP implemented the comma-deletion extension much more generally. We have restricted it in this release to minimize the differences from C99. To get the same effect with both this and previous versions of GCC, the token preceding the special '##' must be a comma, and there must be white space between that comma and whatever comes immediately before it:

```
#define eprintf(format, args...) fprintf (stderr, format , ##args)
```

See Section 11.4 [Differences from previous versions], page 56, for the gory details.

3.7 Predefined Macros

Several object-like macros are predefined; you use them without supplying their definitions. They fall into three classes: standard, common, and system-specific.

In C++, there is a fourth category, the named operators. They act like predefined macros, but you cannot undefine them.

3.7.1 Standard Predefined Macros

The standard predefined macros are specified by the relevant language standards, so they are available with all compilers that implement those standards. Older compilers may not provide all of them. Their names all start with double underscores.

__FILE__   This macro expands to the name of the current input file, in the form of a C string constant. This is the path by which the preprocessor opened the file, not the short name specified in '#include' or as the input file name argument. For example, "/usr/local/include/myheader.h" is a possible expansion of this macro.

__LINE__   This macro expands to the current input line number, in the form of a decimal integer constant. While we call it a predefined macro, it's a pretty strange macro, since its "definition" changes with each new line of source code.

__FILE__ and __LINE__ are useful in generating an error message to report an inconsistency detected by the program; the message can state the source line at which the inconsistency was detected. For example,

```
fprintf (stderr, "Internal error: "
                 "negative string length "
                 "%d at %s, line %d.",
         length, __FILE__, __LINE__);
```

An '#include' directive changes the expansions of __FILE__ and __LINE__ to correspond to the included file. At the end of that file, when processing resumes on the input file that contained the '#include' directive, the expansions of __FILE__ and __LINE__ revert to the values they had before the '#include' (but __LINE__ is then incremented by one as processing moves to the line after the '#include').

A '#line' directive changes __LINE__, and may change __FILE__ as well. See Chapter 6 [Line Control], page 45.

C99 introduces __func__, and GCC has provided __FUNCTION__ for a long time. Both of these are strings containing the name of the current function (there are slight semantic differences; see the GCC manual). Neither of them is a macro; the preprocessor does not know the name of the current function. They tend to be useful in conjunction with __FILE__ and __LINE__, though.

__DATE__   This macro expands to a string constant that describes the date on which the preprocessor is being run. The string constant contains eleven characters and looks like "Feb 12 1996". If the day of the month is less than 10, it is padded with a space on the left.

If GCC cannot determine the current date, it will emit a warning message (once per compilation) and __DATE__ will expand to "??? ?? ????".

__TIME__   This macro expands to a string constant that describes the time at which the preprocessor is being run. The string constant contains eight characters and looks like `"23:59:01"`.

If GCC cannot determine the current time, it will emit a warning message (once per compilation) and `__TIME__` will expand to `"??:??:??"`.

__STDC__   In normal operation, this macro expands to the constant 1, to signify that this compiler conforms to ISO Standard C. If GNU CPP is used with a compiler other than GCC, this is not necessarily true; however, the preprocessor always conforms to the standard unless the '-traditional-cpp' option is used.

This macro is not defined if the '-traditional-cpp' option is used.

On some hosts, the system compiler uses a different convention, where `__STDC__` is normally 0, but is 1 if the user specifies strict conformance to the C Standard. CPP follows the host convention when processing system header files, but when processing user files `__STDC__` is always 1. This has been reported to cause problems; for instance, some versions of Solaris provide X Windows headers that expect `__STDC__` to be either undefined or 1. See Chapter 12 [Invocation], page 57.

__STDC_VERSION__

This macro expands to the C Standard's version number, a long integer constant of the form *yyyymmL* where *yyyy* and *mm* are the year and month of the Standard version. This signifies which version of the C Standard the compiler conforms to. Like `__STDC__`, this is not necessarily accurate for the entire implementation, unless GNU CPP is being used with GCC.

The value `199409L` signifies the 1989 C standard as amended in 1994, which is the current default; the value `199901L` signifies the 1999 revision of the C standard. Support for the 1999 revision is not yet complete.

This macro is not defined if the '-traditional-cpp' option is used, nor when compiling C++ or Objective-C.

__STDC_HOSTED__

This macro is defined, with value 1, if the compiler's target is a *hosted environment*. A hosted environment has the complete facilities of the standard C library available.

__cplusplus

This macro is defined when the C++ compiler is in use. You can use `__cplusplus` to test whether a header is compiled by a C compiler or a C++ compiler. This macro is similar to `__STDC_VERSION__`, in that it expands to a version number. Depending on the language standard selected, the value of the macro is `199711L`, as mandated by the 1998 C++ standard; `201103L`, per the 2011 C++ standard; an unspecified value strictly larger than `201103L` for the experimental languages enabled by '-std=c++1y' and '-std=gnu++1y'.

__OBJC__   This macro is defined, with value 1, when the Objective-C compiler is in use. You can use `__OBJC__` to test whether a header is compiled by a C compiler or an Objective-C compiler.

`__ASSEMBLER__`
> This macro is defined with value 1 when preprocessing assembly language.

3.7.2 Common Predefined Macros

The common predefined macros are GNU C extensions. They are available with the same meanings regardless of the machine or operating system on which you are using GNU C or GNU Fortran. Their names all start with double underscores.

`__COUNTER__`
> This macro expands to sequential integral values starting from 0. In conjunction with the `##` operator, this provides a convenient means to generate unique identifiers. Care must be taken to ensure that `__COUNTER__` is not expanded prior to inclusion of precompiled headers which use it. Otherwise, the precompiled headers will not be used.

`__GFORTRAN__`
> The GNU Fortran compiler defines this.

`__GNUC__`
`__GNUC_MINOR__`
`__GNUC_PATCHLEVEL__`
> These macros are defined by all GNU compilers that use the C preprocessor: C, C++, Objective-C and Fortran. Their values are the major version, minor version, and patch level of the compiler, as integer constants. For example, GCC 3.2.1 will define `__GNUC__` to 3, `__GNUC_MINOR__` to 2, and `__GNUC_PATCHLEVEL__` to 1. These macros are also defined if you invoke the preprocessor directly.
>
> `__GNUC_PATCHLEVEL__` is new to GCC 3.0; it is also present in the widely-used development snapshots leading up to 3.0 (which identify themselves as GCC 2.96 or 2.97, depending on which snapshot you have).
>
> If all you need to know is whether or not your program is being compiled by GCC, or a non-GCC compiler that claims to accept the GNU C dialects, you can simply test `__GNUC__`. If you need to write code which depends on a specific version, you must be more careful. Each time the minor version is increased, the patch level is reset to zero; each time the major version is increased (which happens rarely), the minor version and patch level are reset. If you wish to use the predefined macros directly in the conditional, you will need to write it like this:
> ```
> /* Test for GCC > 3.2.0 */
> #if __GNUC__ > 3 || \
>     (__GNUC__ == 3 && (__GNUC_MINOR__ > 2 || \
>                        (__GNUC_MINOR__ == 2 && \
>                         __GNUC_PATCHLEVEL__ > 0))
> ```
> Another approach is to use the predefined macros to calculate a single number, then compare that against a threshold:
> ```
> #define GCC_VERSION (__GNUC__ * 10000 \
>                      + __GNUC_MINOR__ * 100 \
>                      + __GNUC_PATCHLEVEL__)
>     ...
> ```

```
/* Test for GCC > 3.2.0 */
#if GCC_VERSION > 30200
```

Many people find this form easier to understand.

__GNUG__   The GNU C++ compiler defines this. Testing it is equivalent to testing
            (__GNUC__ && __cplusplus).

__STRICT_ANSI__

            GCC defines this macro if and only if the '-ansi' switch, or a '-std' switch
            specifying strict conformance to some version of ISO C or ISO C++, was specified
            when GCC was invoked. It is defined to '1'. This macro exists primarily to
            direct GNU libc's header files to restrict their definitions to the minimal set
            found in the 1989 C standard.

__BASE_FILE__

            This macro expands to the name of the main input file, in the form of a C string
            constant. This is the source file that was specified on the command line of the
            preprocessor or C compiler.

__INCLUDE_LEVEL__

            This macro expands to a decimal integer constant that represents the depth
            of nesting in include files. The value of this macro is incremented on every
            '#include' directive and decremented at the end of every included file. It
            starts out at 0, its value within the base file specified on the command line.

__ELF__   This macro is defined if the target uses the ELF object format.

__VERSION__

            This macro expands to a string constant which describes the version of the
            compiler in use. You should not rely on its contents having any particular
            form, but it can be counted on to contain at least the release number.

__OPTIMIZE__
__OPTIMIZE_SIZE__
__NO_INLINE__

            These macros describe the compilation mode. __OPTIMIZE__ is defined in all
            optimizing compilations. __OPTIMIZE_SIZE__ is defined if the compiler is op-
            timizing for size, not speed. __NO_INLINE__ is defined if no functions will
            be inlined into their callers (when not optimizing, or when inlining has been
            specifically disabled by '-fno-inline').

            These macros cause certain GNU header files to provide optimized definitions,
            using macros or inline functions, of system library functions. You should not
            use these macros in any way unless you make sure that programs will execute
            with the same effect whether or not they are defined. If they are defined, their
            value is 1.

__GNUC_GNU_INLINE__

            GCC defines this macro if functions declared inline will be handled in GCC's
            traditional gnu90 mode. Object files will contain externally visible definitions of
            all functions declared inline without extern or static. They will not contain
            any definitions of any functions declared extern inline.

__GNUC_STDC_INLINE__

> GCC defines this macro if functions declared `inline` will be handled according to the ISO C99 standard. Object files will contain externally visible definitions of all functions declared `extern inline`. They will not contain definitions of any functions declared `inline` without `extern`.
>
> If this macro is defined, GCC supports the `gnu_inline` function attribute as a way to always get the gnu90 behavior. Support for this and `__GNUC_GNU_INLINE__` was added in GCC 4.1.3. If neither macro is defined, an older version of GCC is being used: `inline` functions will be compiled in gnu90 mode, and the `gnu_inline` function attribute will not be recognized.

__CHAR_UNSIGNED__

> GCC defines this macro if and only if the data type `char` is unsigned on the target machine. It exists to cause the standard header file 'limits.h' to work correctly. You should not use this macro yourself; instead, refer to the standard macros defined in 'limits.h'.

__WCHAR_UNSIGNED__

> Like `__CHAR_UNSIGNED__`, this macro is defined if and only if the data type `wchar_t` is unsigned and the front-end is in C++ mode.

__REGISTER_PREFIX__

> This macro expands to a single token (not a string constant) which is the prefix applied to CPU register names in assembly language for this target. You can use it to write assembly that is usable in multiple environments. For example, in the `m68k-aout` environment it expands to nothing, but in the `m68k-coff` environment it expands to a single '%'.

__USER_LABEL_PREFIX__

> This macro expands to a single token which is the prefix applied to user labels (symbols visible to C code) in assembly. For example, in the `m68k-aout` environment it expands to an '_', but in the `m68k-coff` environment it expands to nothing.
>
> This macro will have the correct definition even if '-f(no-)underscores' is in use, but it will not be correct if target-specific options that adjust this prefix are used (e.g. the OSF/rose '-mno-underscores' option).

```
__SIZE_TYPE__
__PTRDIFF_TYPE__
__WCHAR_TYPE__
__WINT_TYPE__
__INTMAX_TYPE__
__UINTMAX_TYPE__
__SIG_ATOMIC_TYPE__
__INT8_TYPE__
__INT16_TYPE__
__INT32_TYPE__
__INT64_TYPE__
__UINT8_TYPE__
__UINT16_TYPE__
__UINT32_TYPE__
__UINT64_TYPE__
__INT_LEAST8_TYPE__
__INT_LEAST16_TYPE__
__INT_LEAST32_TYPE__
__INT_LEAST64_TYPE__
__UINT_LEAST8_TYPE__
__UINT_LEAST16_TYPE__
__UINT_LEAST32_TYPE__
__UINT_LEAST64_TYPE__
__INT_FAST8_TYPE__
__INT_FAST16_TYPE__
__INT_FAST32_TYPE__
__INT_FAST64_TYPE__
__UINT_FAST8_TYPE__
__UINT_FAST16_TYPE__
__UINT_FAST32_TYPE__
__UINT_FAST64_TYPE__
__INTPTR_TYPE__
__UINTPTR_TYPE__
```

These macros are defined to the correct underlying types for the `size_t`, `ptrdiff_t`, `wchar_t`, `wint_t`, `intmax_t`, `uintmax_t`, `sig_atomic_t`, `int8_t`, `int16_t`, `int32_t`, `int64_t`, `uint8_t`, `uint16_t`, `uint32_t`, `uint64_t`, `int_least8_t`, `int_least16_t`, `int_least32_t`, `int_least64_t`, `uint_least8_t`, `uint_least16_t`, `uint_least32_t`, `uint_least64_t`, `int_fast8_t`, `int_fast16_t`, `int_fast32_t`, `int_fast64_t`, `uint_fast8_t`, `uint_fast16_t`, `uint_fast32_t`, `uint_fast64_t`, `intptr_t`, and `uintptr_t` typedefs, respectively. They exist to make the standard header files 'stddef.h', 'stdint.h', and 'wchar.h' work correctly. You should not use these macros directly; instead, include the appropriate headers and use the typedefs. Some of these macros may not be defined on particular systems if GCC does not provide a 'stdint.h' header on those systems.

__CHAR_BIT__

> Defined to the number of bits used in the representation of the **char** data type.
> It exists to make the standard header given numerical limits work correctly. You
> should not use this macro directly; instead, include the appropriate headers.

```
__SCHAR_MAX__
__WCHAR_MAX__
__SHRT_MAX__
__INT_MAX__
__LONG_MAX__
__LONG_LONG_MAX__
__WINT_MAX__
__SIZE_MAX__
__PTRDIFF_MAX__
__INTMAX_MAX__
__UINTMAX_MAX__
__SIG_ATOMIC_MAX__
__INT8_MAX__
__INT16_MAX__
__INT32_MAX__
__INT64_MAX__
__UINT8_MAX__
__UINT16_MAX__
__UINT32_MAX__
__UINT64_MAX__
__INT_LEAST8_MAX__
__INT_LEAST16_MAX__
__INT_LEAST32_MAX__
__INT_LEAST64_MAX__
__UINT_LEAST8_MAX__
__UINT_LEAST16_MAX__
__UINT_LEAST32_MAX__
__UINT_LEAST64_MAX__
__INT_FAST8_MAX__
__INT_FAST16_MAX__
__INT_FAST32_MAX__
__INT_FAST64_MAX__
__UINT_FAST8_MAX__
__UINT_FAST16_MAX__
__UINT_FAST32_MAX__
__UINT_FAST64_MAX__
__INTPTR_MAX__
__UINTPTR_MAX__
__WCHAR_MIN__
__WINT_MIN__
__SIG_ATOMIC_MIN__
```

Defined to the maximum value of the signed char, wchar_t, signed short, signed int, signed long, signed long long, wint_t, size_t, ptrdiff_t, intmax_t, uintmax_t, sig_atomic_t, int8_t, int16_t, int32_t, int64_t, uint8_t, uint16_t, uint32_t, uint64_t, int_least8_t, int_least16_t, int_least32_t, int_least64_t, uint_least8_t, uint_least16_t, uint_least32_t, uint_least64_t, int_fast8_t, int_fast16_t, int_ fast32_t, int_fast64_t, uint_fast8_t, uint_fast16_t, uint_fast32_t, uint_fast64_t, intptr_t, and uintptr_t types and to the minimum value of the wchar_t, wint_t, and sig_atomic_t types respectively. They exist to make the standard header given numerical limits work correctly. You should not use these macros directly; instead, include the appropriate headers. Some of these macros may not be defined on particular systems if GCC does not provide a 'stdint.h' header on those systems.

__INT8_C
__INT16_C
__INT32_C
__INT64_C
__UINT8_C
__UINT16_C
__UINT32_C
__UINT64_C
__INTMAX_C
__UINTMAX_C

Defined to implementations of the standard 'stdint.h' macros with the same names without the leading __. They exist the make the implementation of that header work correctly. You should not use these macros directly; instead, include the appropriate headers. Some of these macros may not be defined on particular systems if GCC does not provide a 'stdint.h' header on those systems.

__SIZEOF_INT__
__SIZEOF_LONG__
__SIZEOF_LONG_LONG__
__SIZEOF_SHORT__
__SIZEOF_POINTER__
__SIZEOF_FLOAT__
__SIZEOF_DOUBLE__
__SIZEOF_LONG_DOUBLE__
__SIZEOF_SIZE_T__
__SIZEOF_WCHAR_T__
__SIZEOF_WINT_T__
__SIZEOF_PTRDIFF_T__

Defined to the number of bytes of the C standard data types: int, long, long long, short, void *, float, double, long double, size_t, wchar_t, wint_t and ptrdiff_t.

__BYTE_ORDER__
__ORDER_LITTLE_ENDIAN__
__ORDER_BIG_ENDIAN__
__ORDER_PDP_ENDIAN__

__BYTE_ORDER__ is defined to one of the values __ORDER_LITTLE_ENDIAN__, __ORDER_BIG_ENDIAN__, or __ORDER_PDP_ENDIAN__ to reflect the layout of multi-byte and multi-word quantities in memory. If __BYTE_ORDER__ is equal to __ORDER_LITTLE_ENDIAN__ or __ORDER_BIG_ENDIAN__, then multi-byte and multi-word quantities are laid out identically: the byte (word) at the lowest address is the least significant or most significant byte (word) of the quantity, respectively. If `__BYTE_ORDER__` is equal to `__ORDER_PDP_ENDIAN__`, then bytes in 16-bit words are laid out in a little-endian fashion, whereas the 16-bit subwords of a 32-bit quantity are laid out in big-endian fashion.

You should use these macros for testing like this:

```
/* Test for a little-endian machine */
#if __BYTE_ORDER__ == __ORDER_LITTLE_ENDIAN__
```

`__FLOAT_WORD_ORDER__`

> `__FLOAT_WORD_ORDER__` is defined to one of the values `__ORDER_LITTLE_ENDIAN__` or `__ORDER_BIG_ENDIAN__` to reflect the layout of the words of multi-word floating-point quantities.

`__DEPRECATED`

> This macro is defined, with value 1, when compiling a C++ source file with warnings about deprecated constructs enabled. These warnings are enabled by default, but can be disabled with '`-Wno-deprecated`'.

`__EXCEPTIONS`

> This macro is defined, with value 1, when compiling a C++ source file with exceptions enabled. If '`-fno-exceptions`' is used when compiling the file, then this macro is not defined.

`__GXX_RTTI`

> This macro is defined, with value 1, when compiling a C++ source file with runtime type identification enabled. If '`-fno-rtti`' is used when compiling the file, then this macro is not defined.

`__USING_SJLJ_EXCEPTIONS__`

> This macro is defined, with value 1, if the compiler uses the old mechanism based on `setjmp` and `longjmp` for exception handling.

`__GXX_EXPERIMENTAL_CXX0X__`

> This macro is defined when compiling a C++ source file with the option '`-std=c++0x`' or '`-std=gnu++0x`'. It indicates that some features likely to be included in C++0x are available. Note that these features are experimental, and may change or be removed in future versions of GCC.

`__GXX_WEAK__`

> This macro is defined when compiling a C++ source file. It has the value 1 if the compiler will use weak symbols, COMDAT sections, or other similar techniques to collapse symbols with "vague linkage" that are defined in multiple translation units. If the compiler will not collapse such symbols, this macro is defined with value 0. In general, user code should not need to make use of this macro; the purpose of this macro is to ease implementation of the C++ runtime library provided with G++.

`__NEXT_RUNTIME__`

> This macro is defined, with value 1, if (and only if) the NeXT runtime (as in '`-fnext-runtime`') is in use for Objective-C. If the GNU runtime is used,

this macro is not defined, so that you can use this macro to determine which runtime (NeXT or GNU) is being used.

`__LP64__`
`_LP64`   These macros are defined, with value 1, if (and only if) the compilation is for a target where **long int** and pointer both use 64-bits and **int** uses 32-bit.

`__SSP__`   This macro is defined, with value 1, when '-fstack-protector' is in use.

`__SSP_ALL__`
            This macro is defined, with value 2, when '-fstack-protector-all' is in use.

`__SSP_STRONG__`
            This macro is defined, with value 3, when '-fstack-protector-strong' is in use.

`__SSP_EXPLICIT__`
            This macro is defined, with value 4, when '-fstack-protector-explicit' is in use.

`__SANITIZE_ADDRESS__`
            This macro is defined, with value 1, when '-fsanitize=address' or '-fsanitize=kernel-address' are in use.

`__TIMESTAMP__`
            This macro expands to a string constant that describes the date and time of the last modification of the current source file. The string constant contains abbreviated day of the week, month, day of the month, time in hh:mm:ss form, year and looks like `"Sun Sep 16 01:03:52 1973"`. If the day of the month is less than 10, it is padded with a space on the left.

            If GCC cannot determine the current date, it will emit a warning message (once per compilation) and `__TIMESTAMP__` will expand to `"??? ??? ?? ??:??:?? ????"`.

`__GCC_HAVE_SYNC_COMPARE_AND_SWAP_1`
`__GCC_HAVE_SYNC_COMPARE_AND_SWAP_2`
`__GCC_HAVE_SYNC_COMPARE_AND_SWAP_4`
`__GCC_HAVE_SYNC_COMPARE_AND_SWAP_8`
`__GCC_HAVE_SYNC_COMPARE_AND_SWAP_16`
            These macros are defined when the target processor supports atomic compare and swap operations on operands 1, 2, 4, 8 or 16 bytes in length, respectively.

`__GCC_HAVE_DWARF2_CFI_ASM`
            This macro is defined when the compiler is emitting Dwarf2 CFI directives to the assembler. When this is defined, it is possible to emit those same directives in inline assembly.

`__FP_FAST_FMA`
`__FP_FAST_FMAF`
`__FP_FAST_FMAL`
            These macros are defined with value 1 if the backend supports the **fma**, **fmaf**, and **fmal** builtin functions, so that the include file '**math.h**' can define the

macros `FP_FAST_FMA`, `FP_FAST_FMAF`, and `FP_FAST_FMAL` for compatibility with the 1999 C standard.

`__GCC_IEC_559`

This macro is defined to indicate the intended level of support for IEEE 754 (IEC 60559) floating-point arithmetic. It expands to a nonnegative integer value. If 0, it indicates that the combination of the compiler configuration and the command-line options is not intended to support IEEE 754 arithmetic for `float` and `double` as defined in C99 and C11 Annex F (for example, that the standard rounding modes and exceptions are not supported, or that optimizations are enabled that conflict with IEEE 754 semantics). If 1, it indicates that IEEE 754 arithmetic is intended to be supported; this does not mean that all relevant language features are supported by GCC. If 2 or more, it additionally indicates support for IEEE 754-2008 (in particular, that the binary encodings for quiet and signaling NaNs are as specified in IEEE 754-2008).

This macro does not indicate the default state of command-line options that control optimizations that C99 and C11 permit to be controlled by standard pragmas, where those standards do not require a particular default state. It does not indicate whether optimizations respect signaling NaN semantics (the macro for that is `__SUPPORT_SNAN__`). It does not indicate support for decimal floating point or the IEEE 754 binary16 and binary128 types.

`__GCC_IEC_559_COMPLEX`

This macro is defined to indicate the intended level of support for IEEE 754 (IEC 60559) floating-point arithmetic for complex numbers, as defined in C99 and C11 Annex G. It expands to a nonnegative integer value. If 0, it indicates that the combination of the compiler configuration and the command-line options is not intended to support Annex G requirements (for example, because '`-fcx-limited-range`' was used). If 1 or more, it indicates that it is intended to support those requirements; this does not mean that all relevant language features are supported by GCC.

`__NO_MATH_ERRNO__`

This macro is defined if '`-fno-math-errno`' is used, or enabled by another option such as '`-ffast-math`' or by default.

3.7.3 System-specific Predefined Macros

The C preprocessor normally predefines several macros that indicate what type of system and machine is in use. They are obviously different on each target supported by GCC. This manual, being for all systems and machines, cannot tell you what their names are, but you can use `cpp -dM` to see them all. See Chapter 12 [Invocation], page 57. All system-specific predefined macros expand to a constant value, so you can test them with either '`#ifdef`' or '`#if`'.

The C standard requires that all system-specific macros be part of the *reserved namespace*. All names which begin with two underscores, or an underscore and a capital letter, are reserved for the compiler and library to use as they wish. However, historically system-specific macros have had names with no special prefix; for instance, it is common to find `unix` defined on Unix systems. For all such macros, GCC provides a parallel macro with two underscores added at the beginning and the end. If `unix` is defined, `__unix__` will be defined too. There will never be more than two underscores; the parallel of `_mips` is `__mips__`.

When the '`-ansi`' option, or any '`-std`' option that requests strict conformance, is given to the compiler, all the system-specific predefined macros outside the reserved namespace are suppressed. The parallel macros, inside the reserved namespace, remain defined.

We are slowly phasing out all predefined macros which are outside the reserved namespace. You should never use them in new programs, and we encourage you to correct older code to use the parallel macros whenever you find it. We don't recommend you use the system-specific macros that are in the reserved namespace, either. It is better in the long run to check specifically for features you need, using a tool such as `autoconf`.

3.7.4 C++ Named Operators

In C++, there are eleven keywords which are simply alternate spellings of operators normally written with punctuation. These keywords are treated as such even in the preprocessor. They function as operators in '`#if`', and they cannot be defined as macros or poisoned. In C, you can request that those keywords take their C++ meaning by including '`iso646.h`'. That header defines each one as a normal object-like macro expanding to the appropriate punctuator.

These are the named operators and their corresponding punctuators:

Named Operator	Punctuator
and	&&
and_eq	&=
bitand	&
bitor	|
compl	~
not	!
not_eq	!=
or	||
or_eq	|=
xor	^
xor_eq	^=

3.8 Undefining and Redefining Macros

If a macro ceases to be useful, it may be *undefined* with the '`#undef`' directive. '`#undef`' takes a single argument, the name of the macro to undefine. You use the bare macro name, even if the macro is function-like. It is an error if anything appears on the line after the macro name. '`#undef`' has no effect if the name is not a macro.

```
#define FOO 4
x = FOO;        ↦ x = 4;
#undef FOO
x = FOO;        ↦ x = FOO;
```

Once a macro has been undefined, that identifier may be *redefined* as a macro by a subsequent '`#define`' directive. The new definition need not have any resemblance to the old definition.

However, if an identifier which is currently a macro is redefined, then the new definition must be *effectively the same* as the old one. Two macro definitions are effectively the same if:

- Both are the same type of macro (object- or function-like).
- All the tokens of the replacement list are the same.
- If there are any parameters, they are the same.
- Whitespace appears in the same places in both. It need not be exactly the same amount of whitespace, though. Remember that comments count as whitespace.

These definitions are effectively the same:

```
#define FOUR (2 + 2)
#define FOUR         (2    +    2)
#define FOUR (2 /* two */ + 2)
```

but these are not:

```
#define FOUR (2 + 2)
#define FOUR ( 2+2 )
#define FOUR (2 * 2)
#define FOUR(score,and,seven,years,ago) (2 + 2)
```

If a macro is redefined with a definition that is not effectively the same as the old one, the preprocessor issues a warning and changes the macro to use the new definition. If the new definition is effectively the same, the redefinition is silently ignored. This allows, for instance, two different headers to define a common macro. The preprocessor will only complain if the definitions do not match.

3.9 Directives Within Macro Arguments

Occasionally it is convenient to use preprocessor directives within the arguments of a macro. The C and C++ standards declare that behavior in these cases is undefined.

Versions of CPP prior to 3.2 would reject such constructs with an error message. This was the only syntactic difference between normal functions and function-like macros, so it seemed attractive to remove this limitation, and people would often be surprised that they could not use macros in this way. Moreover, sometimes people would use conditional compilation in the argument list to a normal library function like 'printf', only to find that after a library upgrade 'printf' had changed to be a function-like macro, and their code would no longer compile. So from version 3.2 we changed CPP to successfully process arbitrary directives within macro arguments in exactly the same way as it would have processed the directive were the function-like macro invocation not present.

If, within a macro invocation, that macro is redefined, then the new definition takes effect in time for argument pre-expansion, but the original definition is still used for argument replacement. Here is a pathological example:

```
#define f(x) x x
f (1
#undef f
#define f 2
f)
```

which expands to

```
1 2 1 2
```

with the semantics described above.

3.10 Macro Pitfalls

In this section we describe some special rules that apply to macros and macro expansion, and point out certain cases in which the rules have counter-intuitive consequences that you must watch out for.

3.10.1 Misnesting

When a macro is called with arguments, the arguments are substituted into the macro body and the result is checked, together with the rest of the input file, for more macro calls. It is possible to piece together a macro call coming partially from the macro body and partially from the arguments. For example,

```
#define twice(x) (2*(x))
#define call_with_1(x) x(1)
call_with_1 (twice)
      ↦ twice(1)
      ↦ (2*(1))
```

Macro definitions do not have to have balanced parentheses. By writing an unbalanced open parenthesis in a macro body, it is possible to create a macro call that begins inside the macro body but ends outside of it. For example,

```
#define strange(file) fprintf (file, "%s %d",
...
strange(stderr) p, 35)
      ↦ fprintf (stderr, "%s %d", p, 35)
```

The ability to piece together a macro call can be useful, but the use of unbalanced open parentheses in a macro body is just confusing, and should be avoided.

3.10.2 Operator Precedence Problems

You may have noticed that in most of the macro definition examples shown above, each occurrence of a macro argument name had parentheses around it. In addition, another pair of parentheses usually surround the entire macro definition. Here is why it is best to write macros that way.

Suppose you define a macro as follows,

```
#define ceil_div(x, y) (x + y - 1) / y
```

whose purpose is to divide, rounding up. (One use for this operation is to compute how many **int** objects are needed to hold a certain number of **char** objects.) Then suppose it is used as follows:

```
a = ceil_div (b & c, sizeof (int));
      ↦ a = (b & c + sizeof (int) - 1) / sizeof (int);
```

This does not do what is intended. The operator-precedence rules of C make it equivalent to this:

```
a = (b & (c + sizeof (int) - 1)) / sizeof (int);
```

What we want is this:

```
a = ((b & c) + sizeof (int) - 1)) / sizeof (int);
```

Defining the macro as

```
#define ceil_div(x, y) ((x) + (y) - 1) / (y)
```

provides the desired result.

Unintended grouping can result in another way. Consider `sizeof ceil_div(1, 2)`. That has the appearance of a C expression that would compute the size of the type of `ceil_div (1, 2)`, but in fact it means something very different. Here is what it expands to:

```
sizeof ((1) + (2) - 1) / (2)
```

This would take the size of an integer and divide it by two. The precedence rules have put the division outside the `sizeof` when it was intended to be inside.

Parentheses around the entire macro definition prevent such problems. Here, then, is the recommended way to define `ceil_div`:

```
#define ceil_div(x, y) (((x) + (y) - 1) / (y))
```

3.10.3 Swallowing the Semicolon

Often it is desirable to define a macro that expands into a compound statement. Consider, for example, the following macro, that advances a pointer (the argument `p` says where to find it) across whitespace characters:

```
#define SKIP_SPACES(p, limit)    \
{ char *lim = (limit);           \
  while (p < lim) {              \
    if (*p++ != ' ') {          \
      p--; break; }}}
```

Here backslash-newline is used to split the macro definition, which must be a single logical line, so that it resembles the way such code would be laid out if not part of a macro definition.

A call to this macro might be `SKIP_SPACES (p, lim)`. Strictly speaking, the call expands to a compound statement, which is a complete statement with no need for a semicolon to end it. However, since it looks like a function call, it minimizes confusion if you can use it like a function call, writing a semicolon afterward, as in `SKIP_SPACES (p, lim);`

This can cause trouble before `else` statements, because the semicolon is actually a null statement. Suppose you write

```
if (*p != 0)
  SKIP_SPACES (p, lim);
else ...
```

The presence of two statements—the compound statement and a null statement—in between the `if` condition and the `else` makes invalid C code.

The definition of the macro `SKIP_SPACES` can be altered to solve this problem, using a `do ... while` statement. Here is how:

```
#define SKIP_SPACES(p, limit)    \
do { char *lim = (limit);        \
     while (p < lim) {           \
       if (*p++ != ' ') {       \
         p--; break; }}}         \
while (0)
```

Now `SKIP_SPACES (p, lim);` expands into

```
do {...} while (0);
```

which is one statement. The loop executes exactly once; most compilers generate no extra code for it.

3.10.4 Duplication of Side Effects

Many C programs define a macro min, for "minimum", like this:

```
#define min(X, Y)  ((X) < (Y) ? (X) : (Y))
```

When you use this macro with an argument containing a side effect, as shown here,

```
next = min (x + y, foo (z));
```

it expands as follows:

```
next = ((x + y) < (foo (z)) ? (x + y) : (foo (z)));
```

where x + y has been substituted for X and foo (z) for Y.

The function foo is used only once in the statement as it appears in the program, but the expression foo (z) has been substituted twice into the macro expansion. As a result, foo might be called two times when the statement is executed. If it has side effects or if it takes a long time to compute, the results might not be what you intended. We say that min is an *unsafe* macro.

The best solution to this problem is to define min in a way that computes the value of foo (z) only once. The C language offers no standard way to do this, but it can be done with GNU extensions as follows:

```
#define min(X, Y)                \
({ typeof (X) x_ = (X);          \
   typeof (Y) y_ = (Y);          \
   (x_ < y_) ? x_ : y_; })
```

The '({ ... })' notation produces a compound statement that acts as an expression. Its value is the value of its last statement. This permits us to define local variables and assign each argument to one. The local variables have underscores after their names to reduce the risk of conflict with an identifier of wider scope (it is impossible to avoid this entirely). Now each argument is evaluated exactly once.

If you do not wish to use GNU C extensions, the only solution is to be careful when *using* the macro min. For example, you can calculate the value of foo (z), save it in a variable, and use that variable in min:

```
#define min(X, Y)  ((X) < (Y) ? (X) : (Y))
...
{
  int tem = foo (z);
  next = min (x + y, tem);
}
```

(where we assume that foo returns type int).

3.10.5 Self-Referential Macros

A *self-referential* macro is one whose name appears in its definition. Recall that all macro definitions are rescanned for more macros to replace. If the self-reference were considered a use of the macro, it would produce an infinitely large expansion. To prevent this, the self-reference is not considered a macro call. It is passed into the preprocessor output unchanged. Consider an example:

```
#define foo (4 + foo)
```

where foo is also a variable in your program.

Following the ordinary rules, each reference to `foo` will expand into `(4 + foo)`; then this will be rescanned and will expand into `(4 + (4 + foo))`; and so on until the computer runs out of memory.

The self-reference rule cuts this process short after one step, at `(4 + foo)`. Therefore, this macro definition has the possibly useful effect of causing the program to add 4 to the value of `foo` wherever `foo` is referred to.

In most cases, it is a bad idea to take advantage of this feature. A person reading the program who sees that `foo` is a variable will not expect that it is a macro as well. The reader will come across the identifier `foo` in the program and think its value should be that of the variable `foo`, whereas in fact the value is four greater.

One common, useful use of self-reference is to create a macro which expands to itself. If you write

```
#define EPERM EPERM
```

then the macro `EPERM` expands to `EPERM`. Effectively, it is left alone by the preprocessor whenever it's used in running text. You can tell that it's a macro with '`#ifdef`'. You might do this if you want to define numeric constants with an `enum`, but have '`#ifdef`' be true for each constant.

If a macro `x` expands to use a macro `y`, and the expansion of `y` refers to the macro `x`, that is an *indirect self-reference* of `x`. `x` is not expanded in this case either. Thus, if we have

```
#define x (4 + y)
#define y (2 * x)
```

then `x` and `y` expand as follows:

```
x    ↦ (4 + y)
     ↦ (4 + (2 * x))

y    ↦ (2 * x)
     ↦ (2 * (4 + y))
```

Each macro is expanded when it appears in the definition of the other macro, but not when it indirectly appears in its own definition.

3.10.6 Argument Prescan

Macro arguments are completely macro-expanded before they are substituted into a macro body, unless they are stringified or pasted with other tokens. After substitution, the entire macro body, including the substituted arguments, is scanned again for macros to be expanded. The result is that the arguments are scanned *twice* to expand macro calls in them.

Most of the time, this has no effect. If the argument contained any macro calls, they are expanded during the first scan. The result therefore contains no macro calls, so the second scan does not change it. If the argument were substituted as given, with no prescan, the single remaining scan would find the same macro calls and produce the same results.

You might expect the double scan to change the results when a self-referential macro is used in an argument of another macro (see Section 3.10.5 [Self-Referential Macros], page 37): the self-referential macro would be expanded once in the first scan, and a second time in the second scan. However, this is not what happens. The self-references that do not expand in the first scan are marked so that they will not expand in the second scan either.

You might wonder, "Why mention the prescan, if it makes no difference? And why not skip it and make the preprocessor faster?" The answer is that the prescan does make a difference in three special cases:

- Nested calls to a macro.

  We say that *nested* calls to a macro occur when a macro's argument contains a call to that very macro. For example, if `f` is a macro that expects one argument, `f (f (1))` is a nested pair of calls to `f`. The desired expansion is made by expanding `f (1)` and substituting that into the definition of `f`. The prescan causes the expected result to happen. Without the prescan, `f (1)` itself would be substituted as an argument, and the inner use of `f` would appear during the main scan as an indirect self-reference and would not be expanded.

- Macros that call other macros that stringify or concatenate.

  If an argument is stringified or concatenated, the prescan does not occur. If you *want* to expand a macro, then stringify or concatenate its expansion, you can do that by causing one macro to call another macro that does the stringification or concatenation. For instance, if you have

  ```
  #define AFTERX(x) X_ ## x
  #define XAFTERX(x) AFTERX(x)
  #define TABLESIZE 1024
  #define BUFSIZE TABLESIZE
  ```

  then `AFTERX(BUFSIZE)` expands to `X_BUFSIZE`, and `XAFTERX(BUFSIZE)` expands to `X_ 1024`. (Not to `X_TABLESIZE`. Prescan always does a complete expansion.)

- Macros used in arguments, whose expansions contain unshielded commas.

  This can cause a macro expanded on the second scan to be called with the wrong number of arguments. Here is an example:

  ```
  #define foo  a,b
  #define bar(x) lose(x)
  #define lose(x) (1 + (x))
  ```

  We would like `bar(foo)` to turn into `(1 + (foo))`, which would then turn into `(1 + (a,b))`. Instead, `bar(foo)` expands into `lose(a,b)`, and you get an error because `lose` requires a single argument. In this case, the problem is easily solved by the same parentheses that ought to be used to prevent misnesting of arithmetic operations:

  ```
  #define foo (a,b)
  ```

  or

  ```
  #define bar(x) lose((x))
  ```

  The extra pair of parentheses prevents the comma in `foo`'s definition from being interpreted as an argument separator.

3.10.7 Newlines in Arguments

The invocation of a function-like macro can extend over many logical lines. However, in the present implementation, the entire expansion comes out on one line. Thus line numbers emitted by the compiler or debugger refer to the line the invocation started on, which might be different to the line containing the argument causing the problem.

Here is an example illustrating this:

```
#define ignore_second_arg(a,b,c) a; c
```

```
ignore_second_arg (foo (),
                   ignored (),
                   syntax error);
```

The syntax error triggered by the tokens **syntax error** results in an error message citing line three—the line of ignore_second_arg— even though the problematic code comes from line five.

We consider this a bug, and intend to fix it in the near future.

4 Conditionals

A *conditional* is a directive that instructs the preprocessor to select whether or not to include a chunk of code in the final token stream passed to the compiler. Preprocessor conditionals can test arithmetic expressions, or whether a name is defined as a macro, or both simultaneously using the special **defined** operator.

A conditional in the C preprocessor resembles in some ways an **if** statement in C, but it is important to understand the difference between them. The condition in an **if** statement is tested during the execution of your program. Its purpose is to allow your program to behave differently from run to run, depending on the data it is operating on. The condition in a preprocessing conditional directive is tested when your program is compiled. Its purpose is to allow different code to be included in the program depending on the situation at the time of compilation.

However, the distinction is becoming less clear. Modern compilers often do test **if** statements when a program is compiled, if their conditions are known not to vary at run time, and eliminate code which can never be executed. If you can count on your compiler to do this, you may find that your program is more readable if you use **if** statements with constant conditions (perhaps determined by macros). Of course, you can only use this to exclude code, not type definitions or other preprocessing directives, and you can only do it if the code remains syntactically valid when it is not to be used.

GCC version 3 eliminates this kind of never-executed code even when not optimizing. Older versions did it only when optimizing.

4.1 Conditional Uses

There are three general reasons to use a conditional.

- A program may need to use different code depending on the machine or operating system it is to run on. In some cases the code for one operating system may be erroneous on another operating system; for example, it might refer to data types or constants that do not exist on the other system. When this happens, it is not enough to avoid executing the invalid code. Its mere presence will cause the compiler to reject the program. With a preprocessing conditional, the offending code can be effectively excised from the program when it is not valid.

- You may want to be able to compile the same source file into two different programs. One version might make frequent time-consuming consistency checks on its intermediate data, or print the values of those data for debugging, and the other not.

- A conditional whose condition is always false is one way to exclude code from the program but keep it as a sort of comment for future reference.

Simple programs that do not need system-specific logic or complex debugging hooks generally will not need to use preprocessing conditionals.

4.2 Conditional Syntax

A conditional in the C preprocessor begins with a *conditional directive*: '#if', '#ifdef' or '#ifndef'.

4.2.1 Ifdef

The simplest sort of conditional is

```
#ifdef MACRO

controlled text

#endif /* MACRO */
```

This block is called a *conditional group*. *controlled text* will be included in the output of the preprocessor if and only if *MACRO* is defined. We say that the conditional *succeeds* if *MACRO* is defined, *fails* if it is not.

The *controlled text* inside of a conditional can include preprocessing directives. They are executed only if the conditional succeeds. You can nest conditional groups inside other conditional groups, but they must be completely nested. In other words, '#endif' always matches the nearest '#ifdef' (or '#ifndef', or '#if'). Also, you cannot start a conditional group in one file and end it in another.

Even if a conditional fails, the *controlled text* inside it is still run through initial transformations and tokenization. Therefore, it must all be lexically valid C. Normally the only way this matters is that all comments and string literals inside a failing conditional group must still be properly ended.

The comment following the '#endif' is not required, but it is a good practice if there is a lot of *controlled text*, because it helps people match the '#endif' to the corresponding '#ifdef'. Older programs sometimes put *MACRO* directly after the '#endif' without enclosing it in a comment. This is invalid code according to the C standard. CPP accepts it with a warning. It never affects which '#ifndef' the '#endif' matches.

Sometimes you wish to use some code if a macro is *not* defined. You can do this by writing '#ifndef' instead of '#ifdef'. One common use of '#ifndef' is to include code only the first time a header file is included. See Section 2.4 [Once-Only Headers], page 10.

Macro definitions can vary between compilations for several reasons. Here are some samples.

- Some macros are predefined on each kind of machine (see Section 3.7.3 [System-specific Predefined Macros], page 32). This allows you to provide code specially tuned for a particular machine.

- System header files define more macros, associated with the features they implement. You can test these macros with conditionals to avoid using a system feature on a machine where it is not implemented.

- Macros can be defined or undefined with the '-D' and '-U' command-line options when you compile the program. You can arrange to compile the same source file into two different programs by choosing a macro name to specify which program you want, writing conditionals to test whether or how this macro is defined, and then controlling the state of the macro with command-line options, perhaps set in the Makefile. See Chapter 12 [Invocation], page 57.

- Your program might have a special header file (often called 'config.h') that is adjusted when the program is compiled. It can define or not define macros depending on the features of the system and the desired capabilities of the program. The adjustment can be automated by a tool such as autoconf, or done by hand.

4.2.2 If

The '#if' directive allows you to test the value of an arithmetic expression, rather than the mere existence of one macro. Its syntax is

```
#if expression

controlled text

#endif /* expression */
```

expression is a C expression of integer type, subject to stringent restrictions. It may contain

- Integer constants.
- Character constants, which are interpreted as they would be in normal code.
- Arithmetic operators for addition, subtraction, multiplication, division, bitwise operations, shifts, comparisons, and logical operations (&& and ||). The latter two obey the usual short-circuiting rules of standard C.
- Macros. All macros in the expression are expanded before actual computation of the expression's value begins.
- Uses of the defined operator, which lets you check whether macros are defined in the middle of an '#if'.
- Identifiers that are not macros, which are all considered to be the number zero. This allows you to write #if MACRO instead of #ifdef MACRO, if you know that MACRO, when defined, will always have a nonzero value. Function-like macros used without their function call parentheses are also treated as zero.

  In some contexts this shortcut is undesirable. The '-Wundef' option causes GCC to warn whenever it encounters an identifier which is not a macro in an '#if'.

The preprocessor does not know anything about types in the language. Therefore, sizeof operators are not recognized in '#if', and neither are enum constants. They will be taken as identifiers which are not macros, and replaced by zero. In the case of sizeof, this is likely to cause the expression to be invalid.

The preprocessor calculates the value of *expression*. It carries out all calculations in the widest integer type known to the compiler; on most machines supported by GCC this is 64 bits. This is not the same rule as the compiler uses to calculate the value of a constant expression, and may give different results in some cases. If the value comes out to be nonzero, the '#if' succeeds and the *controlled text* is included; otherwise it is skipped.

4.2.3 Defined

The special operator defined is used in '#if' and '#elif' expressions to test whether a certain name is defined as a macro. defined *name* and defined (*name*) are both expressions whose value is 1 if *name* is defined as a macro at the current point in the program, and 0 otherwise. Thus, `#if defined MACRO` is precisely equivalent to `#ifdef MACRO`.

`defined` is useful when you wish to test more than one macro for existence at once. For example,

```
#if defined (__vax__) || defined (__ns16000__)
```

would succeed if either of the names `__vax__` or `__ns16000__` is defined as a macro.

Conditionals written like this:

```
#if defined BUFSIZE && BUFSIZE >= 1024
```

can generally be simplified to just `#if BUFSIZE >= 1024`, since if `BUFSIZE` is not defined, it will be interpreted as having the value zero.

If the `defined` operator appears as a result of a macro expansion, the C standard says the behavior is undefined. GNU cpp treats it as a genuine `defined` operator and evaluates it normally. It will warn wherever your code uses this feature if you use the command-line option '`-pedantic`', since other compilers may handle it differently.

4.2.4 Else

The '`#else`' directive can be added to a conditional to provide alternative text to be used if the condition fails. This is what it looks like:

```
#if expression
text-if-true
#else /* Not expression */
text-if-false
#endif /* Not expression */
```

If *expression* is nonzero, the *text-if-true* is included and the *text-if-false* is skipped. If *expression* is zero, the opposite happens.

You can use '`#else`' with '`#ifdef`' and '`#ifndef`', too.

4.2.5 Elif

One common case of nested conditionals is used to check for more than two possible alternatives. For example, you might have

```
#if X == 1
...
#else /* X != 1 */
#if X == 2
...
#else /* X != 2 */
...
#endif /* X != 2 */
#endif /* X != 1 */
```

Another conditional directive, '`#elif`', allows this to be abbreviated as follows:

```
#if X == 1
...
#elif X == 2
...
#else /* X != 2 and X != 1*/
...
#endif /* X != 2 and X != 1*/
```

'`#elif`' stands for "else if". Like '`#else`', it goes in the middle of a conditional group and subdivides it; it does not require a matching '`#endif`' of its own. Like '`#if`', the '`#elif`' directive includes an expression to be tested. The text following the '#elif' is processed only if the original '#if'-condition failed and the '#elif' condition succeeds.

More than one '#elif' can go in the same conditional group. Then the text after each '#elif' is processed only if the '#elif' condition succeeds after the original '#if' and all previous '#elif' directives within it have failed.

'#else' is allowed after any number of '#elif' directives, but '#elif' may not follow '#else'.

4.3 Deleted Code

If you replace or delete a part of the program but want to keep the old code around for future reference, you often cannot simply comment it out. Block comments do not nest, so the first comment inside the old code will end the commenting-out. The probable result is a flood of syntax errors.

One way to avoid this problem is to use an always-false conditional instead. For instance, put #if 0 before the deleted code and #endif after it. This works even if the code being turned off contains conditionals, but they must be entire conditionals (balanced '#if' and '#endif').

Some people use #ifdef notdef instead. This is risky, because notdef might be accidentally defined as a macro, and then the conditional would succeed. #if 0 can be counted on to fail.

Do not use #if 0 for comments which are not C code. Use a real comment, instead. The interior of #if 0 must consist of complete tokens; in particular, single-quote characters must balance. Comments often contain unbalanced single-quote characters (known in English as apostrophes). These confuse #if 0. They don't confuse '/*'.

5 Diagnostics

The directive '#error' causes the preprocessor to report a fatal error. The tokens forming the rest of the line following '#error' are used as the error message.

You would use '#error' inside of a conditional that detects a combination of parameters which you know the program does not properly support. For example, if you know that the program will not run properly on a VAX, you might write

```
#ifdef __vax__
#error "Won't work on VAXen.  See comments at get_last_object."
#endif
```

If you have several configuration parameters that must be set up by the installation in a consistent way, you can use conditionals to detect an inconsistency and report it with '#error'. For example,

```
#if !defined(FOO) && defined(BAR)
#error "BAR requires FOO."
#endif
```

The directive '#warning' is like '#error', but causes the preprocessor to issue a warning and continue preprocessing. The tokens following '#warning' are used as the warning message.

You might use '#warning' in obsolete header files, with a message directing the user to the header file which should be used instead.

Neither '#error' nor '#warning' macro-expands its argument. Internal whitespace sequences are each replaced with a single space. The line must consist of complete tokens. It is wisest to make the argument of these directives be a single string constant; this avoids problems with apostrophes and the like.

6 Line Control

The C preprocessor informs the C compiler of the location in your source code where each token came from. Presently, this is just the file name and line number. All the tokens resulting from macro expansion are reported as having appeared on the line of the source file where the outermost macro was used. We intend to be more accurate in the future.

If you write a program which generates source code, such as the **bison** parser generator, you may want to adjust the preprocessor's notion of the current file name and line number by hand. Parts of the output from **bison** are generated from scratch, other parts come from a standard parser file. The rest are copied verbatim from **bison**'s input. You would like compiler error messages and symbolic debuggers to be able to refer to **bison**'s input file.

bison or any such program can arrange this by writing '#line' directives into the output file. '#line' is a directive that specifies the original line number and source file name for subsequent input in the current preprocessor input file. '#line' has three variants:

#line *linenum*

> *linenum* is a non-negative decimal integer constant. It specifies the line number which should be reported for the following line of input. Subsequent lines are counted from *linenum*.

#line *linenum filename*

> *linenum* is the same as for the first form, and has the same effect. In addition, *filename* is a string constant. The following line and all subsequent lines are reported to come from the file it specifies, until something else happens to change that. *filename* is interpreted according to the normal rules for a string constant: backslash escapes are interpreted. This is different from '#include'.

> Previous versions of CPP did not interpret escapes in '#line'; we have changed it because the standard requires they be interpreted, and most other compilers do.

#line *anything else*

> *anything else* is checked for macro calls, which are expanded. The result should match one of the above two forms.

'#line' directives alter the results of the __FILE__ and __LINE__ predefined macros from that point on. See Section 3.7.1 [Standard Predefined Macros], page 21. They do not have any effect on '#include''s idea of the directory containing the current file. This is a change from GCC 2.95. Previously, a file reading

```
#line 1 "../src/gram.y"
#include "gram.h"
```

would search for 'gram.h' in '../src', then the '-I' chain; the directory containing the physical source file would not be searched. In GCC 3.0 and later, the '#include' is not affected by the presence of a '#line' referring to a different directory.

We made this change because the old behavior caused problems when generated source files were transported between machines. For instance, it is common practice to ship generated parsers with a source release, so that people building the distribution do not need to have yacc or Bison installed. These files frequently have '#line' directives referring to the directory tree of the system where the distribution was created. If GCC tries to search for headers in those directories, the build is likely to fail.

The new behavior can cause failures too, if the generated file is not in the same directory as its source and it attempts to include a header which would be visible searching from the directory containing the source file. However, this problem is easily solved with an additional '-I' switch on the command line. The failures caused by the old semantics could sometimes be corrected only by editing the generated files, which is difficult and error-prone.

7 Pragmas

The '#pragma' directive is the method specified by the C standard for providing additional information to the compiler, beyond what is conveyed in the language itself. Three forms of this directive (commonly known as *pragmas*) are specified by the 1999 C standard. A C compiler is free to attach any meaning it likes to other pragmas.

GCC has historically preferred to use extensions to the syntax of the language, such as __attribute__, for this purpose. However, GCC does define a few pragmas of its own. These mostly have effects on the entire translation unit or source file.

In GCC version 3, all GNU-defined, supported pragmas have been given a GCC prefix. This is in line with the STDC prefix on all pragmas defined by C99. For backward compatibility, pragmas which were recognized by previous versions are still recognized without the GCC prefix, but that usage is deprecated. Some older pragmas are deprecated in their entirety. They are not recognized with the GCC prefix. See Section 11.3 [Obsolete Features], page 55.

C99 introduces the _Pragma operator. This feature addresses a major problem with '#pragma': being a directive, it cannot be produced as the result of macro expansion. _Pragma is an operator, much like sizeof or defined, and can be embedded in a macro.

Its syntax is _Pragma (*string-literal*), where *string-literal* can be either a normal or wide-character string literal. It is destringized, by replacing all '\\' with a single '\' and all '\"' with a '"'. The result is then processed as if it had appeared as the right hand side of a '#pragma' directive. For example,

```
_Pragma ("GCC dependency \"parse.y\"")
```

has the same effect as #pragma GCC dependency "parse.y". The same effect could be achieved using macros, for example

```
#define DO_PRAGMA(x) _Pragma (#x)
DO_PRAGMA (GCC dependency "parse.y")
```

The standard is unclear on where a _Pragma operator can appear. The preprocessor does not accept it within a preprocessing conditional directive like '#if'. To be safe, you are probably best keeping it out of directives other than '#define', and putting it on a line of its own.

This manual documents the pragmas which are meaningful to the preprocessor itself. Other pragmas are meaningful to the C or C++ compilers. They are documented in the GCC manual.

GCC plugins may provide their own pragmas.

#pragma GCC dependency

> #pragma GCC dependency allows you to check the relative dates of the current file and another file. If the other file is more recent than the current file, a warning is issued. This is useful if the current file is derived from the other file, and should be regenerated. The other file is searched for using the normal include search path. Optional trailing text can be used to give more information in the warning message.
>
> ```
> #pragma GCC dependency "parse.y"
> #pragma GCC dependency "/usr/include/time.h" rerun fixincludes
> ```

#pragma GCC poison

> Sometimes, there is an identifier that you want to remove completely from your program, and make sure that it never creeps back in. To enforce this, you can *poison* the identifier with this pragma. #pragma GCC poison is followed by a list of identifiers to poison. If any of those identifiers appears anywhere in the source after the directive, it is a hard error. For example,
>
> ```
> #pragma GCC poison printf sprintf fprintf
> sprintf(some_string, "hello");
> ```
>
> will produce an error.
>
> If a poisoned identifier appears as part of the expansion of a macro which was defined before the identifier was poisoned, it will *not* cause an error. This lets you poison an identifier without worrying about system headers defining macros that use it.
>
> For example,
>
> ```
> #define strrchr rindex
> #pragma GCC poison rindex
> strrchr(some_string, 'h');
> ```
>
> will not produce an error.

#pragma GCC system_header

> This pragma takes no arguments. It causes the rest of the code in the current file to be treated as if it came from a system header. See Section 2.8 [System Headers], page 13.

#pragma GCC warning
#pragma GCC error

> #pragma GCC warning "message" causes the preprocessor to issue a warning diagnostic with the text 'message'. The message contained in the pragma must be a single string literal. Similarly, #pragma GCC error "message" issues an error message. Unlike the '#warning' and '#error' directives, these pragmas can be embedded in preprocessor macros using '_Pragma'.

8 Other Directives

The '#ident' directive takes one argument, a string constant. On some systems, that string constant is copied into a special segment of the object file. On other systems, the directive is ignored. The '#sccs' directive is a synonym for '#ident'.

These directives are not part of the C standard, but they are not official GNU extensions either. What historical information we have been able to find, suggests they originated with System V.

The *null directive* consists of a '#' followed by a newline, with only whitespace (including comments) in between. A null directive is understood as a preprocessing directive but has no effect on the preprocessor output. The primary significance of the existence of the null directive is that an input line consisting of just a '#' will produce no output, rather than a line of output containing just a '#'. Supposedly some old C programs contain such lines.

9 Preprocessor Output

When the C preprocessor is used with the C, C++, or Objective-C compilers, it is integrated into the compiler and communicates a stream of binary tokens directly to the compiler's parser. However, it can also be used in the more conventional standalone mode, where it produces textual output.

The output from the C preprocessor looks much like the input, except that all preprocessing directive lines have been replaced with blank lines and all comments with spaces. Long runs of blank lines are discarded.

The ISO standard specifies that it is implementation defined whether a preprocessor preserves whitespace between tokens, or replaces it with e.g. a single space. In GNU CPP, whitespace between tokens is collapsed to become a single space, with the exception that the first token on a non-directive line is preceded with sufficient spaces that it appears in the same column in the preprocessed output that it appeared in the original source file. This is so the output is easy to read. See Section 11.4 [Differences from previous versions], page 56. CPP does not insert any whitespace where there was none in the original source, except where necessary to prevent an accidental token paste.

Source file name and line number information is conveyed by lines of the form

```
# linenum filename flags
```

These are called *linemarkers*. They are inserted as needed into the output (but never within a string or character constant). They mean that the following line originated in file *filename* at line *linenum*. *filename* will never contain any non-printing characters; they are replaced with octal escape sequences.

After the file name comes zero or more flags, which are '1', '2', '3', or '4'. If there are multiple flags, spaces separate them. Here is what the flags mean:

'1'   This indicates the start of a new file.

'2'   This indicates returning to a file (after having included another file).

'3'   This indicates that the following text comes from a system header file, so certain warnings should be suppressed.

'4'   This indicates that the following text should be treated as being wrapped in an implicit `extern "C"` block.

As an extension, the preprocessor accepts linemarkers in non-assembler input files. They are treated like the corresponding '#line' directive, (see Chapter 6 [Line Control], page 45), except that trailing flags are permitted, and are interpreted with the meanings described above. If multiple flags are given, they must be in ascending order.

Some directives may be duplicated in the output of the preprocessor. These are '#ident' (always), '#pragma' (only if the preprocessor does not handle the pragma itself), and '#define' and '#undef' (with certain debugging options). If this happens, the '#' of the directive will always be in the first column, and there will be no space between the '#' and the directive name. If macro expansion happens to generate tokens which might be mistaken for a duplicated directive, a space will be inserted between the '#' and the directive name.

10 Traditional Mode

Traditional (pre-standard) C preprocessing is rather different from the preprocessing specified by the standard. When GCC is given the '-traditional-cpp' option, it attempts to emulate a traditional preprocessor.

GCC versions 3.2 and later only support traditional mode semantics in the preprocessor, and not in the compiler front ends. This chapter outlines the traditional preprocessor semantics we implemented.

The implementation does not correspond precisely to the behavior of earlier versions of GCC, nor to any true traditional preprocessor. After all, inconsistencies among traditional implementations were a major motivation for C standardization. However, we intend that it should be compatible with true traditional preprocessors in all ways that actually matter.

10.1 Traditional lexical analysis

The traditional preprocessor does not decompose its input into tokens the same way a standards-conforming preprocessor does. The input is simply treated as a stream of text with minimal internal form.

This implementation does not treat trigraphs (see [trigraphs], page 2) specially since they were an invention of the standards committee. It handles arbitrarily-positioned escaped newlines properly and splices the lines as you would expect; many traditional preprocessors did not do this.

The form of horizontal whitespace in the input file is preserved in the output. In particular, hard tabs remain hard tabs. This can be useful if, for example, you are preprocessing a Makefile.

Traditional CPP only recognizes C-style block comments, and treats the '/*' sequence as introducing a comment only if it lies outside quoted text. Quoted text is introduced by the usual single and double quotes, and also by an initial '<' in a `#include` directive.

Traditionally, comments are completely removed and are not replaced with a space. Since a traditional compiler does its own tokenization of the output of the preprocessor, this means that comments can effectively be used as token paste operators. However, comments behave like separators for text handled by the preprocessor itself, since it doesn't re-lex its input. For example, in

```
#if foo/**/bar
```

'foo' and 'bar' are distinct identifiers and expanded separately if they happen to be macros. In other words, this directive is equivalent to

```
#if foo bar
```

rather than

```
#if foobar
```

Generally speaking, in traditional mode an opening quote need not have a matching closing quote. In particular, a macro may be defined with replacement text that contains an unmatched quote. Of course, if you attempt to compile preprocessed output containing an unmatched quote you will get a syntax error.

However, all preprocessing directives other than **#define** require matching quotes. For example:

```
#define m This macro's fine and has an unmatched quote
"/* This is not a comment.  */
/* This is a comment.  The following #include directive
   is ill-formed.  */
#include <stdio.h
```

Just as for the ISO preprocessor, what would be a closing quote can be escaped with a backslash to prevent the quoted text from closing.

10.2 Traditional macros

The major difference between traditional and ISO macros is that the former expand to text rather than to a token sequence. CPP removes all leading and trailing horizontal whitespace from a macro's replacement text before storing it, but preserves the form of internal whitespace.

One consequence is that it is legitimate for the replacement text to contain an unmatched quote (see Section 10.1 [Traditional lexical analysis], page 49). An unclosed string or character constant continues into the text following the macro call. Similarly, the text at the end of a macro's expansion can run together with the text after the macro invocation to produce a single token.

Normally comments are removed from the replacement text after the macro is expanded, but if the '-CC' option is passed on the command-line comments are preserved. (In fact, the current implementation removes comments even before saving the macro replacement text, but it careful to do it in such a way that the observed effect is identical even in the function-like macro case.)

The ISO stringification operator '#' and token paste operator '##' have no special meaning. As explained later, an effect similar to these operators can be obtained in a different way. Macro names that are embedded in quotes, either from the main file or after macro replacement, do not expand.

CPP replaces an unquoted object-like macro name with its replacement text, and then rescans it for further macros to replace. Unlike standard macro expansion, traditional macro expansion has no provision to prevent recursion. If an object-like macro appears unquoted in its replacement text, it will be replaced again during the rescan pass, and so on *ad infinitum.* GCC detects when it is expanding recursive macros, emits an error message, and continues after the offending macro invocation.

```
#define PLUS +
#define INC(x) PLUS+x
INC(foo);
      ↦ ++foo;
```

Function-like macros are similar in form but quite different in behavior to their ISO counterparts. Their arguments are contained within parentheses, are comma-separated, and can cross physical lines. Commas within nested parentheses are not treated as argument separators. Similarly, a quote in an argument cannot be left unclosed; a following comma or parenthesis that comes before the closing quote is treated like any other character. There is no facility for handling variadic macros.

This implementation removes all comments from macro arguments, unless the '-C' option is given. The form of all other horizontal whitespace in arguments is preserved, including leading and trailing whitespace. In particular

```
f( )
```

is treated as an invocation of the macro 'f' with a single argument consisting of a single space. If you want to invoke a function-like macro that takes no arguments, you must not leave any whitespace between the parentheses.

If a macro argument crosses a new line, the new line is replaced with a space when forming the argument. If the previous line contained an unterminated quote, the following line inherits the quoted state.

Traditional preprocessors replace parameters in the replacement text with their arguments regardless of whether the parameters are within quotes or not. This provides a way to stringize arguments. For example

```
#define str(x) "x"
str(/* A comment */some text )
      ↦ "some text "
```

Note that the comment is removed, but that the trailing space is preserved. Here is an example of using a comment to effect token pasting.

```
#define suffix(x) foo_/**/x
suffix(bar)
      ↦ foo_bar
```

10.3 Traditional miscellany

Here are some things to be aware of when using the traditional preprocessor.

- Preprocessing directives are recognized only when their leading '#' appears in the first column. There can be no whitespace between the beginning of the line and the '#', but whitespace can follow the '#'.

- A true traditional C preprocessor does not recognize '#error' or '#pragma', and may not recognize '#elif'. CPP supports all the directives in traditional mode that it supports in ISO mode, including extensions, with the exception that the effects of '#pragma GCC poison' are undefined.

- __STDC__ is not defined.

- If you use digraphs the behavior is undefined.

- If a line that looks like a directive appears within macro arguments, the behavior is undefined.

10.4 Traditional warnings

You can request warnings about features that did not exist, or worked differently, in traditional C with the '-Wtraditional' option. GCC does not warn about features of ISO C which you must use when you are using a conforming compiler, such as the '#' and '##' operators.

Presently '-Wtraditional' warns about:

- Macro parameters that appear within string literals in the macro body. In traditional C macro replacement takes place within string literals, but does not in ISO C.

- In traditional C, some preprocessor directives did not exist. Traditional preprocessors would only consider a line to be a directive if the '#' appeared in column 1 on the line. Therefore '-Wtraditional' warns about directives that traditional C understands but would ignore because the '#' does not appear as the first character on the line. It also suggests you hide directives like '#pragma' not understood by traditional C by indenting them. Some traditional implementations would not recognize '#elif', so it suggests avoiding it altogether.

- A function-like macro that appears without an argument list. In some traditional preprocessors this was an error. In ISO C it merely means that the macro is not expanded.

- The unary plus operator. This did not exist in traditional C.

- The 'U' and 'LL' integer constant suffixes, which were not available in traditional C. (Traditional C does support the 'L' suffix for simple long integer constants.) You are not warned about uses of these suffixes in macros defined in system headers. For instance, UINT_MAX may well be defined as 4294967295U, but you will not be warned if you use UINT_MAX.

  You can usually avoid the warning, and the related warning about constants which are so large that they are unsigned, by writing the integer constant in question in hexadecimal, with no U suffix. Take care, though, because this gives the wrong result in exotic cases.

11 Implementation Details

Here we document details of how the preprocessor's implementation affects its user-visible behavior. You should try to avoid undue reliance on behavior described here, as it is possible that it will change subtly in future implementations.

Also documented here are obsolete features and changes from previous versions of CPP.

11.1 Implementation-defined behavior

This is how CPP behaves in all the cases which the C standard describes as *implementation-defined*. This term means that the implementation is free to do what it likes, but must document its choice and stick to it.

- The mapping of physical source file multi-byte characters to the execution character set.

  The input character set can be specified using the '-finput-charset' option, while the execution character set may be controlled using the '-fexec-charset' and '-fwide-exec-charset' options.

- Identifier characters.

  The C and C++ standards allow identifiers to be composed of '_' and the alphanumeric characters. C++ and C99 also allow universal character names, and C99 further permits implementation-defined characters.

  GCC allows the '$' character in identifiers as an extension for most targets. This is true regardless of the 'std=' switch, since this extension cannot conflict with standards-conforming programs. When preprocessing assembler, however, dollars are not identifier characters by default.

  Currently the targets that by default do not permit '$' are AVR, IP2K, MMIX, MIPS Irix 3, ARM aout, and PowerPC targets for the AIX operating system.

  You can override the default with '-fdollars-in-identifiers' or 'fno-dollars-in-identifiers'. See [fdollars-in-identifiers], page 64.

- Non-empty sequences of whitespace characters.

  In textual output, each whitespace sequence is collapsed to a single space. For aesthetic reasons, the first token on each non-directive line of output is preceded with sufficient spaces that it appears in the same column as it did in the original source file.

- The numeric value of character constants in preprocessor expressions.

  The preprocessor and compiler interpret character constants in the same way; i.e. escape sequences such as '\a' are given the values they would have on the target machine.

  The compiler evaluates a multi-character character constant a character at a time, shifting the previous value left by the number of bits per target character, and then or-ing in the bit-pattern of the new character truncated to the width of a target character. The final bit-pattern is given type `int`, and is therefore signed, regardless of whether single characters are signed or not (a slight change from versions 3.1 and earlier of GCC). If there are more characters in the constant than would fit in the target `int` the compiler issues a warning, and the excess leading characters are ignored.

  For example, 'ab' for a target with an 8-bit `char` would be interpreted as '(int) ((unsigned char) 'a' * 256 + (unsigned char) 'b')', and '\234a' as '(int) ((unsigned char) '\234' * 256 + (unsigned char) 'a')'.

- Source file inclusion.

  For a discussion on how the preprocessor locates header files, Section 2.2 [Include Operation], page 8.

- Interpretation of the filename resulting from a macro-expanded '#include' directive.
  See Section 2.6 [Computed Includes], page 11.

- Treatment of a '#pragma' directive that after macro-expansion results in a standard pragma.

  No macro expansion occurs on any '#pragma' directive line, so the question does not arise.

Note that GCC does not yet implement any of the standard pragmas.

11.2 Implementation limits

CPP has a small number of internal limits. This section lists the limits which the C standard requires to be no lower than some minimum, and all the others known. It is intended that there should be as few limits as possible. If you encounter an undocumented or inconvenient limit, please report that as a bug. See Section "Reporting Bugs" in *Using the GNU Compiler Collection (GCC)*.

Where we say something is limited *only by available memory*, that means that internal data structures impose no intrinsic limit, and space is allocated with `malloc` or equivalent. The actual limit will therefore depend on many things, such as the size of other things allocated by the compiler at the same time, the amount of memory consumed by other processes on the same computer, etc.

- Nesting levels of '`#include`' files.

  We impose an arbitrary limit of 200 levels, to avoid runaway recursion. The standard requires at least 15 levels.

- Nesting levels of conditional inclusion.

  The C standard mandates this be at least 63. CPP is limited only by available memory.

- Levels of parenthesized expressions within a full expression.

  The C standard requires this to be at least 63. In preprocessor conditional expressions, it is limited only by available memory.

- Significant initial characters in an identifier or macro name.

  The preprocessor treats all characters as significant. The C standard requires only that the first 63 be significant.

- Number of macros simultaneously defined in a single translation unit.

  The standard requires at least 4095 be possible. CPP is limited only by available memory.

- Number of parameters in a macro definition and arguments in a macro call.

  We allow `USHRT_MAX`, which is no smaller than 65,535. The minimum required by the standard is 127.

- Number of characters on a logical source line.

  The C standard requires a minimum of 4096 be permitted. CPP places no limits on this, but you may get incorrect column numbers reported in diagnostics for lines longer than 65,535 characters.

- Maximum size of a source file.

  The standard does not specify any lower limit on the maximum size of a source file. GNU cpp maps files into memory, so it is limited by the available address space. This is generally at least two gigabytes. Depending on the operating system, the size of physical memory may or may not be a limitation.

11.3 Obsolete Features

CPP has some features which are present mainly for compatibility with older programs. We discourage their use in new code. In some cases, we plan to remove the feature in a future version of GCC.

11.3.1 Assertions

Assertions are a deprecated alternative to macros in writing conditionals to test what sort of computer or system the compiled program will run on. Assertions are usually predefined, but you can define them with preprocessing directives or command-line options.

Assertions were intended to provide a more systematic way to describe the compiler's target system and we added them for compatibility with existing compilers. In practice they are just as unpredictable as the system-specific predefined macros. In addition, they are not part of any standard, and only a few compilers support them. Therefore, the use of assertions is **less** portable than the use of system-specific predefined macros. We recommend you do not use them at all.

An assertion looks like this:

```
#predicate (answer)
```

predicate must be a single identifier. *answer* can be any sequence of tokens; all characters are significant except for leading and trailing whitespace, and differences in internal whitespace sequences are ignored. (This is similar to the rules governing macro redefinition.) Thus, (x + y) is different from (x+y) but equivalent to (x + y). Parentheses do not nest inside an answer.

To test an assertion, you write it in an '#if'. For example, this conditional succeeds if either **vax** or **ns16000** has been asserted as an answer for **machine**.

```
#if #machine (vax) || #machine (ns16000)
```

You can test whether *any* answer is asserted for a predicate by omitting the answer in the conditional:

```
#if #machine
```

Assertions are made with the '**#assert**' directive. Its sole argument is the assertion to make, without the leading '**#**' that identifies assertions in conditionals.

```
#assert predicate (answer)
```

You may make several assertions with the same predicate and different answers. Subsequent assertions do not override previous ones for the same predicate. All the answers for any given predicate are simultaneously true.

Assertions can be canceled with the '**#unassert**' directive. It has the same syntax as '**#assert**'. In that form it cancels only the answer which was specified on the '**#unassert**' line; other answers for that predicate remain true. You can cancel an entire predicate by leaving out the answer:

```
#unassert predicate
```

In either form, if no such assertion has been made, '**#unassert**' has no effect.

You can also make or cancel assertions using command-line options. See Chapter 12 [Invocation], page 57.

11.4 Differences from previous versions

This section details behavior which has changed from previous versions of CPP. We do not plan to change it again in the near future, but we do not promise not to, either.

The "previous versions" discussed here are 2.95 and before. The behavior of GCC 3.0 is mostly the same as the behavior of the widely used 2.96 and 2.97 development snapshots. Where there are differences, they generally represent bugs in the snapshots.

- -I- deprecated

  This option has been deprecated in 4.0. '-iquote' is meant to replace the need for this option.

- Order of evaluation of '#' and '##' operators

  The standard does not specify the order of evaluation of a chain of '##' operators, nor whether '#' is evaluated before, after, or at the same time as '##'. You should therefore not write any code which depends on any specific ordering. It is possible to guarantee an ordering, if you need one, by suitable use of nested macros.

  An example of where this might matter is pasting the arguments '1', 'e' and '-2'. This would be fine for left-to-right pasting, but right-to-left pasting would produce an invalid token 'e-2'.

  GCC 3.0 evaluates '#' and '##' at the same time and strictly left to right. Older versions evaluated all '#' operators first, then all '##' operators, in an unreliable order.

- The form of whitespace between tokens in preprocessor output

  See Chapter 9 [Preprocessor Output], page 48, for the current textual format. This is also the format used by stringification. Normally, the preprocessor communicates tokens directly to the compiler's parser, and whitespace does not come up at all.

  Older versions of GCC preserved all whitespace provided by the user and inserted lots more whitespace of their own, because they could not accurately predict when extra spaces were needed to prevent accidental token pasting.

- Optional argument when invoking rest argument macros

  As an extension, GCC permits you to omit the variable arguments entirely when you use a variable argument macro. This is forbidden by the 1999 C standard, and will provoke a pedantic warning with GCC 3.0. Previous versions accepted it silently.

- '##' swallowing preceding text in rest argument macros

  Formerly, in a macro expansion, if '##' appeared before a variable arguments parameter, and the set of tokens specified for that argument in the macro invocation was empty, previous versions of CPP would back up and remove the preceding sequence of non-whitespace characters (**not** the preceding token). This extension is in direct conflict with the 1999 C standard and has been drastically pared back.

  In the current version of the preprocessor, if '##' appears between a comma and a variable arguments parameter, and the variable argument is omitted entirely, the comma will be removed from the expansion. If the variable argument is empty, or the token before '##' is not a comma, then '##' behaves as a normal token paste.

- '#line' and '#include'

  The '#line' directive used to change GCC's notion of the "directory containing the current file", used by '#include' with a double-quoted header file name. In 3.0 and later, it does not. See Chapter 6 [Line Control], page 45, for further explanation.

- Syntax of '#line'

  In GCC 2.95 and previous, the string constant argument to '#line' was treated the same way as the argument to '#include': backslash escapes were not honored, and the string ended at the second '"'. This is not compliant with the C standard. In GCC 3.0, an attempt was made to correct the behavior, so that the string was treated as a real string constant, but it turned out to be buggy. In 3.1, the bugs have been fixed. (We are not fixing the bugs in 3.0 because they affect relatively few people and the fix is quite invasive.)

12 Invocation

Most often when you use the C preprocessor you will not have to invoke it explicitly: the C compiler will do so automatically. However, the preprocessor is sometimes useful on its own. All the options listed here are also acceptable to the C compiler and have the same meaning, except that the C compiler has different rules for specifying the output file.

Note: Whether you use the preprocessor by way of gcc or cpp, the *compiler driver* is run first. This program's purpose is to translate your command into invocations of the programs that do the actual work. Their command-line interfaces are similar but not identical to the documented interface, and may change without notice.

The C preprocessor expects two file names as arguments, *infile* and *outfile*. The preprocessor reads *infile* together with any other files it specifies with '#include'. All the output generated by the combined input files is written in *outfile*.

Either *infile* or *outfile* may be '-', which as *infile* means to read from standard input and as *outfile* means to write to standard output. Also, if either file is omitted, it means the same as if '-' had been specified for that file.

Unless otherwise noted, or the option ends in '=', all options which take an argument may have that argument appear either immediately after the option, or with a space between option and argument: '-Ifoo' and '-I foo' have the same effect.

Many options have multi-letter names; therefore multiple single-letter options may *not* be grouped: '-dM' is very different from '-d -M'.

-D *name*   Predefine *name* as a macro, with definition 1.

-D *name=definition*

                The contents of *definition* are tokenized and processed as if they appeared during translation phase three in a '#define' directive. In particular, the definition will be truncated by embedded newline characters.

                If you are invoking the preprocessor from a shell or shell-like program you may need to use the shell's quoting syntax to protect characters such as spaces that have a meaning in the shell syntax.

                If you wish to define a function-like macro on the command line, write its argument list with surrounding parentheses before the equals sign (if any).

Parentheses are meaningful to most shells, so you will need to quote the option. With `sh` and `csh`, '-D'`name(args...)=definition`'' works.

'-D' and '-U' options are processed in the order they are given on the command line. All '-imacros *file*' and '-include *file*' options are processed after all '-D' and '-U' options.

-U *name*   Cancel any previous definition of *name*, either built in or provided with a '-D' option.

-undef   Do not predefine any system-specific or GCC-specific macros. The standard predefined macros remain defined. See Section 3.7.1 [Standard Predefined Macros], page 21.

-I *dir*   Add the directory *dir* to the list of directories to be searched for header files. See Section 2.3 [Search Path], page 9. Directories named by '-I' are searched before the standard system include directories. If the directory *dir* is a standard system include directory, the option is ignored to ensure that the default search order for system directories and the special treatment of system headers are not defeated (see Section 2.8 [System Headers], page 13) . If *dir* begins with =, then the = will be replaced by the sysroot prefix; see '--sysroot' and '-isysroot'.

-o *file*   Write output to *file*. This is the same as specifying *file* as the second non-option argument to `cpp`. `gcc` has a different interpretation of a second non-option argument, so you must use '-o' to specify the output file.

-Wall   Turns on all optional warnings which are desirable for normal code. At present this is '-Wcomment', '-Wtrigraphs', '-Wmultichar' and a warning about integer promotion causing a change of sign in `#if` expressions. Note that many of the preprocessor's warnings are on by default and have no options to control them.

-Wcomment
-Wcomments
               Warn whenever a comment-start sequence '/*' appears in a '/*' comment, or whenever a backslash-newline appears in a '//' comment. (Both forms have the same effect.)

-Wtrigraphs
               Most trigraphs in comments cannot affect the meaning of the program. However, a trigraph that would form an escaped newline ('??/' at the end of a line) can, by changing where the comment begins or ends. Therefore, only trigraphs that would form escaped newlines produce warnings inside a comment.

               This option is implied by '-Wall'. If '-Wall' is not given, this option is still enabled unless trigraphs are enabled. To get trigraph conversion without warnings, but get the other '-Wall' warnings, use '-trigraphs -Wall -Wno-trigraphs'.

-Wtraditional
               Warn about certain constructs that behave differently in traditional and ISO C. Also warn about ISO C constructs that have no traditional C equivalent, and problematic constructs which should be avoided. See Chapter 10 [Traditional Mode], page 49.

-Wundef   Warn whenever an identifier which is not a macro is encountered in an '#if' directive, outside of 'defined'. Such identifiers are replaced with zero.

-Wunused-macros

Warn about macros defined in the main file that are unused. A macro is *used* if it is expanded or tested for existence at least once. The preprocessor will also warn if the macro has not been used at the time it is redefined or undefined.

Built-in macros, macros defined on the command line, and macros defined in include files are not warned about.

Note: If a macro is actually used, but only used in skipped conditional blocks, then CPP will report it as unused. To avoid the warning in such a case, you might improve the scope of the macro's definition by, for example, moving it into the first skipped block. Alternatively, you could provide a dummy use with something like:

```
#if defined the_macro_causing_the_warning
#endif
```

-Wendif-labels

Warn whenever an '#else' or an '#endif' are followed by text. This usually happens in code of the form

```
#if FOO
...
#else FOO
...
#endif FOO
```

The second and third FOO should be in comments, but often are not in older programs. This warning is on by default.

-Werror   Make all warnings into hard errors. Source code which triggers warnings will be rejected.

-Wsystem-headers

Issue warnings for code in system headers. These are normally unhelpful in finding bugs in your own code, therefore suppressed. If you are responsible for the system library, you may want to see them.

-w   Suppress all warnings, including those which GNU CPP issues by default.

-pedantic

Issue all the mandatory diagnostics listed in the C standard. Some of them are left out by default, since they trigger frequently on harmless code.

-pedantic-errors

Issue all the mandatory diagnostics, and make all mandatory diagnostics into errors. This includes mandatory diagnostics that GCC issues without '-pedantic' but treats as warnings.

-M   Instead of outputting the result of preprocessing, output a rule suitable for **make** describing the dependencies of the main source file. The preprocessor outputs one **make** rule containing the object file name for that source file, a colon, and the names of all the included files, including those coming from '-include' or '-imacros' command-line options.

Unless specified explicitly (with '-MT' or '-MQ'), the object file name consists of the name of the source file with any suffix replaced with object file suffix and with any leading directory parts removed. If there are many included files then the rule is split into several lines using '\'-newline. The rule has no commands.

This option does not suppress the preprocessor's debug output, such as '-dM'. To avoid mixing such debug output with the dependency rules you should explicitly specify the dependency output file with '-MF', or use an environment variable like DEPENDENCIES_OUTPUT (see Chapter 13 [Environment Variables], page 67). Debug output will still be sent to the regular output stream as normal.

Passing '-M' to the driver implies '-E', and suppresses warnings with an implicit '-w'.

-MM   Like '-M' but do not mention header files that are found in system header directories, nor header files that are included, directly or indirectly, from such a header.

           This implies that the choice of angle brackets or double quotes in an '#include' directive does not in itself determine whether that header will appear in '-MM' dependency output. This is a slight change in semantics from GCC versions 3.0 and earlier.

-MF *file* When used with '-M' or '-MM', specifies a file to write the dependencies to. If no '-MF' switch is given the preprocessor sends the rules to the same place it would have sent preprocessed output.

           When used with the driver options '-MD' or '-MMD', '-MF' overrides the default dependency output file.

-MG   In conjunction with an option such as '-M' requesting dependency generation, '-MG' assumes missing header files are generated files and adds them to the dependency list without raising an error. The dependency filename is taken directly from the #include directive without prepending any path. '-MG' also suppresses preprocessed output, as a missing header file renders this useless.

           This feature is used in automatic updating of makefiles.

-MP   This option instructs CPP to add a phony target for each dependency other than the main file, causing each to depend on nothing. These dummy rules work around errors make gives if you remove header files without updating the 'Makefile' to match.

           This is typical output:

           ```
           test.o: test.c test.h

           test.h:
           ```

-MT *target*
           Change the target of the rule emitted by dependency generation. By default CPP takes the name of the main input file, deletes any directory components and any file suffix such as '.c', and appends the platform's usual object suffix. The result is the target.

An '-MT' option will set the target to be exactly the string you specify. If you want multiple targets, you can specify them as a single argument to '-MT', or use multiple '-MT' options.

For example, '-MT '$(objpfx)foo.o'' might give

```
$(objpfx)foo.o: foo.c
```

-MQ *target*

Same as '-MT', but it quotes any characters which are special to Make. '-MQ '$(objpfx)foo.o'' gives

```
$$(objpfx)foo.o: foo.c
```

The default target is automatically quoted, as if it were given with '-MQ'.

-MD

'-MD' is equivalent to '-M -MF *file*', except that '-E' is not implied. The driver determines *file* based on whether an '-o' option is given. If it is, the driver uses its argument but with a suffix of '.d', otherwise it takes the name of the input file, removes any directory components and suffix, and applies a '.d' suffix.

If '-MD' is used in conjunction with '-E', any '-o' switch is understood to specify the dependency output file (see [-MF], page 60), but if used without '-E', each '-o' is understood to specify a target object file.

Since '-E' is not implied, '-MD' can be used to generate a dependency output file as a side-effect of the compilation process.

-MMD

Like '-MD' except mention only user header files, not system header files.

-x c
-x c++
-x objective-c
-x assembler-with-cpp

Specify the source language: C, C++, Objective-C, or assembly. This has nothing to do with standards conformance or extensions; it merely selects which base syntax to expect. If you give none of these options, cpp will deduce the language from the extension of the source file: '.c', '.cc', '.m', or '.S'. Some other common extensions for C++ and assembly are also recognized. If cpp does not recognize the extension, it will treat the file as C; this is the most generic mode.

Note: Previous versions of cpp accepted a '-lang' option which selected both the language and the standards conformance level. This option has been removed, because it conflicts with the '-l' option.

-std=*standard*
-ansi

Specify the standard to which the code should conform. Currently CPP knows about C and C++ standards; others may be added in the future.

standard may be one of:

c90
c89
iso9899:1990

The ISO C standard from 1990. 'c90' is the customary shorthand for this version of the standard.

The '-ansi' option is equivalent to '-std=c90'.

iso9899:199409
> The 1990 C standard, as amended in 1994.

iso9899:1999
c99
iso9899:199x
c9x
> The revised ISO C standard, published in December 1999. Before publication, this was known as C9X.

iso9899:2011
c11
c1x
> The revised ISO C standard, published in December 2011. Before publication, this was known as C1X.

gnu90
gnu89
> The 1990 C standard plus GNU extensions. This is the default.

gnu99
gnu9x
> The 1999 C standard plus GNU extensions.

gnu11
gnu1x
> The 2011 C standard plus GNU extensions.

c++98
> The 1998 ISO C++ standard plus amendments.

gnu++98
> The same as '-std=c++98' plus GNU extensions. This is the default for C++ code.

-I-
> Split the include path. Any directories specified with '-I' options before '-I-' are searched only for headers requested with #include "file"; they are not searched for #include <file>. If additional directories are specified with '-I' options after the '-I-', those directories are searched for all '#include' directives.
>
> In addition, '-I-' inhibits the use of the directory of the current file directory as the first search directory for #include "file". See Section 2.3 [Search Path], page 9. This option has been deprecated.

-nostdinc
> Do not search the standard system directories for header files. Only the directories you have specified with '-I' options (and the directory of the current file, if appropriate) are searched.

-nostdinc++
> Do not search for header files in the C++-specific standard directories, but do still search the other standard directories. (This option is used when building the C++ library.)

-include file
> Process file as if #include "file" appeared as the first line of the primary source file. However, the first directory searched for file is the preprocessor's working directory instead of the directory containing the main source file. If

not found there, it is searched for in the remainder of the #include "..." search chain as normal.

If multiple '-include' options are given, the files are included in the order they appear on the command line.

-imacros *file*

> Exactly like '-include', except that any output produced by scanning *file* is thrown away. Macros it defines remain defined. This allows you to acquire all the macros from a header without also processing its declarations.
>
> All files specified by '-imacros' are processed before all files specified by '-include'.

-idirafter *dir*

> Search *dir* for header files, but do it *after* all directories specified with '-I' and the standard system directories have been exhausted. *dir* is treated as a system include directory. If *dir* begins with =, then the = will be replaced by the sysroot prefix; see '--sysroot' and '-isysroot'.

-iprefix *prefix*

> Specify *prefix* as the prefix for subsequent '-iwithprefix' options. If the prefix represents a directory, you should include the final '/'.

-iwithprefix *dir*
-iwithprefixbefore *dir*

> Append *dir* to the prefix specified previously with '-iprefix', and add the resulting directory to the include search path. '-iwithprefixbefore' puts it in the same place '-I' would; '-iwithprefix' puts it where '-idirafter' would.

-isysroot *dir*

> This option is like the '--sysroot' option, but applies only to header files (except for Darwin targets, where it applies to both header files and libraries). See the '--sysroot' option for more information.

-imultilib *dir*

> Use *dir* as a subdirectory of the directory containing target-specific C++ headers.

-isystem *dir*

> Search *dir* for header files, after all directories specified by '-I' but before the standard system directories. Mark it as a system directory, so that it gets the same special treatment as is applied to the standard system directories. See Section 2.8 [System Headers], page 13. If *dir* begins with =, then the = will be replaced by the sysroot prefix; see '--sysroot' and '-isysroot'.

-iquote *dir*

> Search *dir* only for header files requested with #include "*file*"; they are not searched for #include <*file*>, before all directories specified by '-I' and before the standard system directories. See Section 2.3 [Search Path], page 9. If *dir* begins with =, then the = will be replaced by the sysroot prefix; see '--sysroot' and '-isysroot'.

-fdirectives-only

> When preprocessing, handle directives, but do not expand macros.

The option's behavior depends on the '-E' and '-fpreprocessed' options.

With '-E', preprocessing is limited to the handling of directives such as #define, #ifdef, and #error. Other preprocessor operations, such as macro expansion and trigraph conversion are not performed. In addition, the '-dD' option is implicitly enabled.

With '-fpreprocessed', predefinition of command line and most builtin macros is disabled. Macros such as __LINE__, which are contextually dependent, are handled normally. This enables compilation of files previously preprocessed with -E -fdirectives-only.

With both '-E' and '-fpreprocessed', the rules for '-fpreprocessed' take precedence. This enables full preprocessing of files previously preprocessed with -E -fdirectives-only.

-fdollars-in-identifiers

Accept '$' in identifiers. See [Identifier characters], page 53.

-fextended-identifiers

Accept universal character names in identifiers. This option is enabled by default for C99 (and later C standard versions) and C++.

-fno-canonical-system-headers

When preprocessing, do not shorten system header paths with canonicalization.

-fpreprocessed

Indicate to the preprocessor that the input file has already been preprocessed. This suppresses things like macro expansion, trigraph conversion, escaped newline splicing, and processing of most directives. The preprocessor still recognizes and removes comments, so that you can pass a file preprocessed with '-C' to the compiler without problems. In this mode the integrated preprocessor is little more than a tokenizer for the front ends.

'-fpreprocessed' is implicit if the input file has one of the extensions '.i', '.ii' or '.mi'. These are the extensions that GCC uses for preprocessed files created by '-save-temps'.

-ftabstop=*width*

Set the distance between tab stops. This helps the preprocessor report correct column numbers in warnings or errors, even if tabs appear on the line. If the value is less than 1 or greater than 100, the option is ignored. The default is 8.

-fdebug-cpp

This option is only useful for debugging GCC. When used with '-E', dumps debugging information about location maps. Every token in the output is preceded by the dump of the map its location belongs to. The dump of the map holding the location of a token would be:

```
{'P':'/file/path';'F':'/includer/path';'L':line_num;'C':col_num;'S':system_header_p;'M'
```

When used without '-E', this option has no effect.

-ftrack-macro-expansion[=*level*]

Track locations of tokens across macro expansions. This allows the compiler to emit diagnostic about the current macro expansion stack when a compilation error occurs in a macro expansion. Using this option makes the preprocessor and the compiler consume more memory. The *level* parameter can be used to choose the level of precision of token location tracking thus decreasing the memory consumption if necessary. Value '0' of *level* de-activates this option just as if no '-ftrack-macro-expansion' was present on the command line. Value '1' tracks tokens locations in a degraded mode for the sake of minimal memory overhead. In this mode all tokens resulting from the expansion of an argument of a function-like macro have the same location. Value '2' tracks tokens locations completely. This value is the most memory hungry. When this option is given no argument, the default parameter value is '2'.

Note that -ftrack-macro-expansion=2 is activated by default.

-fexec-charset=*charset*

Set the execution character set, used for string and character constants. The default is UTF-8. *charset* can be any encoding supported by the system's iconv library routine.

-fwide-exec-charset=*charset*

Set the wide execution character set, used for wide string and character constants. The default is UTF-32 or UTF-16, whichever corresponds to the width of wchar_t. As with '-fexec-charset', *charset* can be any encoding supported by the system's iconv library routine; however, you will have problems with encodings that do not fit exactly in wchar_t.

-finput-charset=*charset*

Set the input character set, used for translation from the character set of the input file to the source character set used by GCC. If the locale does not specify, or GCC cannot get this information from the locale, the default is UTF-8. This can be overridden by either the locale or this command-line option. Currently the command-line option takes precedence if there's a conflict. *charset* can be any encoding supported by the system's iconv library routine.

-fworking-directory

Enable generation of linemarkers in the preprocessor output that will let the compiler know the current working directory at the time of preprocessing. When this option is enabled, the preprocessor will emit, after the initial linemarker, a second linemarker with the current working directory followed by two slashes. GCC will use this directory, when it's present in the preprocessed input, as the directory emitted as the current working directory in some debugging information formats. This option is implicitly enabled if debugging information is enabled, but this can be inhibited with the negated form '-fno-working-directory'. If the '-P' flag is present in the command line, this option has no effect, since no #line directives are emitted whatsoever.

-fno-show-column

Do not print column numbers in diagnostics. This may be necessary if diagnostics are being scanned by a program that does not understand the column numbers, such as dejagnu.

-A *predicate=answer*

Make an assertion with the predicate *predicate* and answer *answer*. This form is preferred to the older form '-A *predicate(answer)*', which is still supported, because it does not use shell special characters. See Section 11.3 [Obsolete Features], page 55.

-A *-predicate=answer*

Cancel an assertion with the predicate *predicate* and answer *answer*.

-dCHARS   *CHARS* is a sequence of one or more of the following characters, and must not be preceded by a space. Other characters are interpreted by the compiler proper, or reserved for future versions of GCC, and so are silently ignored. If you specify characters whose behavior conflicts, the result is undefined.

'M'   Instead of the normal output, generate a list of '#define' directives for all the macros defined during the execution of the preprocessor, including predefined macros. This gives you a way of finding out what is predefined in your version of the preprocessor. Assuming you have no file 'foo.h', the command

                               touch foo.h; cpp -dM foo.h

                will show all the predefined macros.

                If you use '-dM' without the '-E' option, '-dM' is interpreted as a synonym for '-fdump-rtl-mach'. See Section "Debugging Options" in gcc.

'D'   Like 'M' except in two respects: it does *not* include the predefined macros, and it outputs *both* the '#define' directives and the result of preprocessing. Both kinds of output go to the standard output file.

'N'   Like 'D', but emit only the macro names, not their expansions.

'I'   Output '#include' directives in addition to the result of preprocessing.

'U'   Like 'D' except that only macros that are expanded, or whose definedness is tested in preprocessor directives, are output; the output is delayed until the use or test of the macro; and '#undef' directives are also output for macros tested but undefined at the time.

-P   Inhibit generation of linemarkers in the output from the preprocessor. This might be useful when running the preprocessor on something that is not C code, and will be sent to a program which might be confused by the linemarkers. See Chapter 9 [Preprocessor Output], page 48.

-C   Do not discard comments. All comments are passed through to the output file, except for comments in processed directives, which are deleted along with the directive.

              You should be prepared for side effects when using '-C'; it causes the preprocessor to treat comments as tokens in their own right. For example, comments appearing at the start of what would be a directive line have the effect of turning that line into an ordinary source line, since the first token on the line is no longer a '#'.

-CC   Do not discard comments, including during macro expansion. This is like '-C', except that comments contained within macros are also passed through to the output file where the macro is expanded.

In addition to the side-effects of the '-C' option, the '-CC' option causes all C++-style comments inside a macro to be converted to C-style comments. This is to prevent later use of that macro from inadvertently commenting out the remainder of the source line.

The '-CC' option is generally used to support lint comments.

-traditional-cpp
        Try to imitate the behavior of old-fashioned C preprocessors, as opposed to ISO C preprocessors. See Chapter 10 [Traditional Mode], page 49.

-trigraphs
        Process trigraph sequences. See Section 1.2 [Initial processing], page 2.

-remap   Enable special code to work around file systems which only permit very short file names, such as MS-DOS.

--help
--target-help
        Print text describing all the command-line options instead of preprocessing anything.

-v   Verbose mode. Print out GNU CPP's version number at the beginning of execution, and report the final form of the include path.

-H   Print the name of each header file used, in addition to other normal activities. Each name is indented to show how deep in the '#include' stack it is. Precompiled header files are also printed, even if they are found to be invalid; an invalid precompiled header file is printed with '...x' and a valid one with '...!'.

-version
--version
        Print out GNU CPP's version number. With one dash, proceed to preprocess as normal. With two dashes, exit immediately.

13 Environment Variables

This section describes the environment variables that affect how CPP operates. You can use them to specify directories or prefixes to use when searching for include files, or to control dependency output.

Note that you can also specify places to search using options such as '-I', and control dependency output with options like '-M' (see Chapter 12 [Invocation], page 57). These take precedence over environment variables, which in turn take precedence over the configuration of GCC.

CPATH
C_INCLUDE_PATH
CPLUS_INCLUDE_PATH
OBJC_INCLUDE_PATH

Each variable's value is a list of directories separated by a special character, much like PATH, in which to look for header files. The special character, PATH_SEPARATOR, is target-dependent and determined at GCC build time. For Microsoft Windows-based targets it is a semicolon, and for almost all other targets it is a colon.

CPATH specifies a list of directories to be searched as if specified with '-I', but after any paths given with '-I' options on the command line. This environment variable is used regardless of which language is being preprocessed.

The remaining environment variables apply only when preprocessing the particular language indicated. Each specifies a list of directories to be searched as if specified with '-isystem', but after any paths given with '-isystem' options on the command line.

In all these variables, an empty element instructs the compiler to search its current working directory. Empty elements can appear at the beginning or end of a path. For instance, if the value of CPATH is :/special/include, that has the same effect as '-I. -I/special/include'.

See also Section 2.3 [Search Path], page 9.

DEPENDENCIES_OUTPUT

If this variable is set, its value specifies how to output dependencies for Make based on the non-system header files processed by the compiler. System header files are ignored in the dependency output.

The value of DEPENDENCIES_OUTPUT can be just a file name, in which case the Make rules are written to that file, guessing the target name from the source file name. Or the value can have the form '*file target*', in which case the rules are written to file *file* using *target* as the target name.

In other words, this environment variable is equivalent to combining the options '-MM' and '-MF' (see Chapter 12 [Invocation], page 57), with an optional '-MT' switch too.

SUNPRO_DEPENDENCIES

This variable is the same as DEPENDENCIES_OUTPUT (see above), except that system header files are not ignored, so it implies '-M' rather than '-MM'. However, the dependence on the main input file is omitted. See Chapter 12 [Invocation], page 57.

GNU Free Documentation License

Version 1.3, 3 November 2008

Copyright © 2000, 2001, 2002, 2007, 2008 Free Software Foundation, Inc.
http://fsf.org/

Everyone is permitted to copy and distribute verbatim copies
of this license document, but changing it is not allowed.

0. PREAMBLE

The purpose of this License is to make a manual, textbook, or other functional and useful document *free* in the sense of freedom: to assure everyone the effective freedom to copy and redistribute it, with or without modifying it, either commercially or non-commercially. Secondarily, this License preserves for the author and publisher a way to get credit for their work, while not being considered responsible for modifications made by others.

This License is a kind of "copyleft", which means that derivative works of the document must themselves be free in the same sense. It complements the GNU General Public License, which is a copyleft license designed for free software.

We have designed this License in order to use it for manuals for free software, because free software needs free documentation: a free program should come with manuals providing the same freedoms that the software does. But this License is not limited to software manuals; it can be used for any textual work, regardless of subject matter or whether it is published as a printed book. We recommend this License principally for works whose purpose is instruction or reference.

1. APPLICABILITY AND DEFINITIONS

This License applies to any manual or other work, in any medium, that contains a notice placed by the copyright holder saying it can be distributed under the terms of this License. Such a notice grants a world-wide, royalty-free license, unlimited in duration, to use that work under the conditions stated herein. The "Document", below, refers to any such manual or work. Any member of the public is a licensee, and is addressed as "you". You accept the license if you copy, modify or distribute the work in a way requiring permission under copyright law.

A "Modified Version" of the Document means any work containing the Document or a portion of it, either copied verbatim, or with modifications and/or translated into another language.

A "Secondary Section" is a named appendix or a front-matter section of the Document that deals exclusively with the relationship of the publishers or authors of the Document to the Document's overall subject (or to related matters) and contains nothing that could fall directly within that overall subject. (Thus, if the Document is in part a textbook of mathematics, a Secondary Section may not explain any mathematics.) The relationship could be a matter of historical connection with the subject or with related matters, or of legal, commercial, philosophical, ethical or political position regarding them.

The "Invariant Sections" are certain Secondary Sections whose titles are designated, as being those of Invariant Sections, in the notice that says that the Document is released under this License. If a section does not fit the above definition of Secondary then it is not allowed to be designated as Invariant. The Document may contain zero Invariant Sections. If the Document does not identify any Invariant Sections then there are none.

The "Cover Texts" are certain short passages of text that are listed, as Front-Cover Texts or Back-Cover Texts, in the notice that says that the Document is released under this License. A Front-Cover Text may be at most 5 words, and a Back-Cover Text may be at most 25 words.

A "Transparent" copy of the Document means a machine-readable copy, represented in a format whose specification is available to the general public, that is suitable for revising the document straightforwardly with generic text editors or (for images composed of pixels) generic paint programs or (for drawings) some widely available drawing editor, and that is suitable for input to text formatters or for automatic translation to a variety of formats suitable for input to text formatters. A copy made in an otherwise Transparent file format whose markup, or absence of markup, has been arranged to thwart or discourage subsequent modification by readers is not Transparent. An image format is not Transparent if used for any substantial amount of text. A copy that is not "Transparent" is called "Opaque".

Examples of suitable formats for Transparent copies include plain ASCII without markup, Texinfo input format, LaTeX input format, SGML or XML using a publicly available DTD, and standard-conforming simple HTML, PostScript or PDF designed for human modification. Examples of transparent image formats include PNG, XCF and JPG. Opaque formats include proprietary formats that can be read and edited only by proprietary word processors, SGML or XML for which the DTD and/or processing tools are not generally available, and the machine-generated HTML, PostScript or PDF produced by some word processors for output purposes only.

The "Title Page" means, for a printed book, the title page itself, plus such following pages as are needed to hold, legibly, the material this License requires to appear in the title page. For works in formats which do not have any title page as such, "Title Page" means the text near the most prominent appearance of the work's title, preceding the beginning of the body of the text.

The "publisher" means any person or entity that distributes copies of the Document to the public.

A section "Entitled XYZ" means a named subunit of the Document whose title either is precisely XYZ or contains XYZ in parentheses following text that translates XYZ in another language. (Here XYZ stands for a specific section name mentioned below, such as "Acknowledgements", "Dedications", "Endorsements", or "History".) To "Preserve the Title" of such a section when you modify the Document means that it remains a section "Entitled XYZ" according to this definition.

The Document may include Warranty Disclaimers next to the notice which states that this License applies to the Document. These Warranty Disclaimers are considered to be included by reference in this License, but only as regards disclaiming warranties: any other implication that these Warranty Disclaimers may have is void and has no effect on the meaning of this License.

2. VERBATIM COPYING

You may copy and distribute the Document in any medium, either commercially or noncommercially, provided that this License, the copyright notices, and the license notice saying this License applies to the Document are reproduced in all copies, and that you add no other conditions whatsoever to those of this License. You may not use technical measures to obstruct or control the reading or further copying of the copies you make or distribute. However, you may accept compensation in exchange for copies. If you distribute a large enough number of copies you must also follow the conditions in section 3.

You may also lend copies, under the same conditions stated above, and you may publicly display copies.

3. COPYING IN QUANTITY

If you publish printed copies (or copies in media that commonly have printed covers) of the Document, numbering more than 100, and the Document's license notice requires Cover Texts, you must enclose the copies in covers that carry, clearly and legibly, all these Cover Texts: Front-Cover Texts on the front cover, and Back-Cover Texts on the back cover. Both covers must also clearly and legibly identify you as the publisher of these copies. The front cover must present the full title with all words of the title equally prominent and visible. You may add other material on the covers in addition. Copying with changes limited to the covers, as long as they preserve the title of the Document and satisfy these conditions, can be treated as verbatim copying in other respects.

If the required texts for either cover are too voluminous to fit legibly, you should put the first ones listed (as many as fit reasonably) on the actual cover, and continue the rest onto adjacent pages.

If you publish or distribute Opaque copies of the Document numbering more than 100, you must either include a machine-readable Transparent copy along with each Opaque copy, or state in or with each Opaque copy a computer-network location from which the general network-using public has access to download using public-standard network protocols a complete Transparent copy of the Document, free of added material. If you use the latter option, you must take reasonably prudent steps, when you begin distribution of Opaque copies in quantity, to ensure that this Transparent copy will remain thus accessible at the stated location until at least one year after the last time you distribute an Opaque copy (directly or through your agents or retailers) of that edition to the public.

It is requested, but not required, that you contact the authors of the Document well before redistributing any large number of copies, to give them a chance to provide you with an updated version of the Document.

4. MODIFICATIONS

You may copy and distribute a Modified Version of the Document under the conditions of sections 2 and 3 above, provided that you release the Modified Version under precisely this License, with the Modified Version filling the role of the Document, thus licensing distribution and modification of the Modified Version to whoever possesses a copy of it. In addition, you must do these things in the Modified Version:

A. Use in the Title Page (and on the covers, if any) a title distinct from that of the Document, and from those of previous versions (which should, if there were any, be listed in the History section of the Document). You may use the same title as a previous version if the original publisher of that version gives permission.

B. List on the Title Page, as authors, one or more persons or entities responsible for authorship of the modifications in the Modified Version, together with at least five of the principal authors of the Document (all of its principal authors, if it has fewer than five), unless they release you from this requirement.

C. State on the Title page the name of the publisher of the Modified Version, as the publisher.

D. Preserve all the copyright notices of the Document.

E. Add an appropriate copyright notice for your modifications adjacent to the other copyright notices.

F. Include, immediately after the copyright notices, a license notice giving the public permission to use the Modified Version under the terms of this License, in the form shown in the Addendum below.

G. Preserve in that license notice the full lists of Invariant Sections and required Cover Texts given in the Document's license notice.

H. Include an unaltered copy of this License.

I. Preserve the section Entitled "History", Preserve its Title, and add to it an item stating at least the title, year, new authors, and publisher of the Modified Version as given on the Title Page. If there is no section Entitled "History" in the Document, create one stating the title, year, authors, and publisher of the Document as given on its Title Page, then add an item describing the Modified Version as stated in the previous sentence.

J. Preserve the network location, if any, given in the Document for public access to a Transparent copy of the Document, and likewise the network locations given in the Document for previous versions it was based on. These may be placed in the "History" section. You may omit a network location for a work that was published at least four years before the Document itself, or if the original publisher of the version it refers to gives permission.

K. For any section Entitled "Acknowledgements" or "Dedications", Preserve the Title of the section, and preserve in the section all the substance and tone of each of the contributor acknowledgements and/or dedications given therein.

L. Preserve all the Invariant Sections of the Document, unaltered in their text and in their titles. Section numbers or the equivalent are not considered part of the section titles.

M. Delete any section Entitled "Endorsements". Such a section may not be included in the Modified Version.

N. Do not retitle any existing section to be Entitled "Endorsements" or to conflict in title with any Invariant Section.

O. Preserve any Warranty Disclaimers.

If the Modified Version includes new front-matter sections or appendices that qualify as Secondary Sections and contain no material copied from the Document, you may at your option designate some or all of these sections as invariant. To do this, add their titles to the list of Invariant Sections in the Modified Version's license notice. These titles must be distinct from any other section titles.

You may add a section Entitled "Endorsements", provided it contains nothing but endorsements of your Modified Version by various parties—for example, statements of peer review or that the text has been approved by an organization as the authoritative definition of a standard.

You may add a passage of up to five words as a Front-Cover Text, and a passage of up to 25 words as a Back-Cover Text, to the end of the list of Cover Texts in the Modified Version. Only one passage of Front-Cover Text and one of Back-Cover Text may be added by (or through arrangements made by) any one entity. If the Document already includes a cover text for the same cover, previously added by you or by arrangement made by the same entity you are acting on behalf of, you may not add another; but you may replace the old one, on explicit permission from the previous publisher that added the old one.

The author(s) and publisher(s) of the Document do not by this License give permission to use their names for publicity for or to assert or imply endorsement of any Modified Version.

5. COMBINING DOCUMENTS

You may combine the Document with other documents released under this License, under the terms defined in section 4 above for modified versions, provided that you include in the combination all of the Invariant Sections of all of the original documents, unmodified, and list them all as Invariant Sections of your combined work in its license notice, and that you preserve all their Warranty Disclaimers.

The combined work need only contain one copy of this License, and multiple identical Invariant Sections may be replaced with a single copy. If there are multiple Invariant Sections with the same name but different contents, make the title of each such section unique by adding at the end of it, in parentheses, the name of the original author or publisher of that section if known, or else a unique number. Make the same adjustment to the section titles in the list of Invariant Sections in the license notice of the combined work.

In the combination, you must combine any sections Entitled "History" in the various original documents, forming one section Entitled "History"; likewise combine any sections Entitled "Acknowledgements", and any sections Entitled "Dedications". You must delete all sections Entitled "Endorsements."

6. COLLECTIONS OF DOCUMENTS

You may make a collection consisting of the Document and other documents released under this License, and replace the individual copies of this License in the various documents with a single copy that is included in the collection, provided that you follow the rules of this License for verbatim copying of each of the documents in all other respects.

You may extract a single document from such a collection, and distribute it individually under this License, provided you insert a copy of this License into the extracted document, and follow this License in all other respects regarding verbatim copying of that document.

7. AGGREGATION WITH INDEPENDENT WORKS

A compilation of the Document or its derivatives with other separate and independent documents or works, in or on a volume of a storage or distribution medium, is called an "aggregate" if the copyright resulting from the compilation is not used to limit the legal rights of the compilation's users beyond what the individual works permit. When the Document is included in an aggregate, this License does not apply to the other works in the aggregate which are not themselves derivative works of the Document.

If the Cover Text requirement of section 3 is applicable to these copies of the Document, then if the Document is less than one half of the entire aggregate, the Document's Cover Texts may be placed on covers that bracket the Document within the aggregate, or the electronic equivalent of covers if the Document is in electronic form. Otherwise they must appear on printed covers that bracket the whole aggregate.

8. TRANSLATION

Translation is considered a kind of modification, so you may distribute translations of the Document under the terms of section 4. Replacing Invariant Sections with translations requires special permission from their copyright holders, but you may include translations of some or all Invariant Sections in addition to the original versions of these Invariant Sections. You may include a translation of this License, and all the license notices in the Document, and any Warranty Disclaimers, provided that you also include the original English version of this License and the original versions of those notices and disclaimers. In case of a disagreement between the translation and the original version of this License or a notice or disclaimer, the original version will prevail.

If a section in the Document is Entitled "Acknowledgements", "Dedications", or "History", the requirement (section 4) to Preserve its Title (section 1) will typically require changing the actual title.

9. TERMINATION

You may not copy, modify, sublicense, or distribute the Document except as expressly provided under this License. Any attempt otherwise to copy, modify, sublicense, or distribute it is void, and will automatically terminate your rights under this License.

However, if you cease all violation of this License, then your license from a particular copyright holder is reinstated (a) provisionally, unless and until the copyright holder explicitly and finally terminates your license, and (b) permanently, if the copyright holder fails to notify you of the violation by some reasonable means prior to 60 days after the cessation.

Moreover, your license from a particular copyright holder is reinstated permanently if the copyright holder notifies you of the violation by some reasonable means, this is the first time you have received notice of violation of this License (for any work) from that copyright holder, and you cure the violation prior to 30 days after your receipt of the notice.

Termination of your rights under this section does not terminate the licenses of parties who have received copies or rights from you under this License. If your rights have been terminated and not permanently reinstated, receipt of a copy of some or all of the same material does not give you any rights to use it.

10. FUTURE REVISIONS OF THIS LICENSE

The Free Software Foundation may publish new, revised versions of the GNU Free Documentation License from time to time. Such new versions will be similar in spirit to the present version, but may differ in detail to address new problems or concerns. See http://www.gnu.org/copyleft/.

Each version of the License is given a distinguishing version number. If the Document specifies that a particular numbered version of this License "or any later version" applies to it, you have the option of following the terms and conditions either of that specified version or of any later version that has been published (not as a draft) by the Free Software Foundation. If the Document does not specify a version number of this License, you may choose any version ever published (not as a draft) by the Free Software Foundation. If the Document specifies that a proxy can decide which future versions of this License can be used, that proxy's public statement of acceptance of a version permanently authorizes you to choose that version for the Document.

11. RELICENSING

"Massive Multiauthor Collaboration Site" (or "MMC Site") means any World Wide Web server that publishes copyrightable works and also provides prominent facilities for anybody to edit those works. A public wiki that anybody can edit is an example of such a server. A "Massive Multiauthor Collaboration" (or "MMC") contained in the site means any set of copyrightable works thus published on the MMC site.

"CC-BY-SA" means the Creative Commons Attribution-Share Alike 3.0 license published by Creative Commons Corporation, a not-for-profit corporation with a principal place of business in San Francisco, California, as well as future copyleft versions of that license published by that same organization.

"Incorporate" means to publish or republish a Document, in whole or in part, as part of another Document.

An MMC is "eligible for relicensing" if it is licensed under this License, and if all works that were first published under this License somewhere other than this MMC, and subsequently incorporated in whole or in part into the MMC, (1) had no cover texts or invariant sections, and (2) were thus incorporated prior to November 1, 2008.

The operator of an MMC Site may republish an MMC contained in the site under CC-BY-SA on the same site at any time before August 1, 2009, provided the MMC is eligible for relicensing.

ADDENDUM: How to use this License for your documents

To use this License in a document you have written, include a copy of the License in the document and put the following copyright and license notices just after the title page:

```
Copyright (C)  year  your name.
Permission is granted to copy, distribute and/or modify this document
under the terms of the GNU Free Documentation License, Version 1.3
or any later version published by the Free Software Foundation;
with no Invariant Sections, no Front-Cover Texts, and no Back-Cover
Texts.  A copy of the license is included in the section entitled ''GNU
Free Documentation License''.
```

If you have Invariant Sections, Front-Cover Texts and Back-Cover Texts, replace the "with...Texts." line with this:

```
with the Invariant Sections being list their titles, with
the Front-Cover Texts being list, and with the Back-Cover Texts
being list.
```

If you have Invariant Sections without Cover Texts, or some other combination of the three, merge those two alternatives to suit the situation.

If your document contains nontrivial examples of program code, we recommend releasing these examples in parallel under your choice of free software license, such as the GNU General Public License, to permit their use in free software.

Index of Directives

Option Index

CPP's command-line options and environment variables are indexed here without any initial '-' or '--'.

Concept Index

www.ingramcontent.com/pod-product-compliance
Lightning Source LLC
LaVergne TN
LVHW082128070326
832902LV00040B/2985